In It for the Long Haul

Building Effective Long-Term Pastorates

Glenn E. Ludwig

An Alban Institute Publication

Scriptural quotations, unless otherwise noted, are from the New Revised Standard Version of the Bible, copyright © 1989, Division of Christian Education of the National Council of the Churches of Christ in the United States of America and are used by permission.

Library of Congress Catalog Card Number 2002109030

ISBN 1-56699-269-9

Dedicated to
Stella
in appreciation for her love and support for
"the long haul"

CONTENTS

Along the Jericho Road in the wilderness of Judea I was surprised to find a rather large flock of sheep—and some goats—grazing as they were able along the barren hillside. In the midst of the flock stood several who appeared to be shepherds. Some distance away, I found a small knoll and I sat for a while. The lengthening shadows announced the late afternoon hour.

As I watched, there was a sudden cry, something of a warbling sound. Some might have said it was a scream. It appeared to come from one of the shepherds. No one seemed to notice! Yet, as I watched, one of the shepherds walked from the center of the large grazing flock and out from its midst. One by one, some of the sheep—but clearly not all—followed. They formed a single line moving out and over the next hill.

There were no yipping dogs herding the sheep. No one checked to see that each sheep bore the brand of the "Double Aleph Ranch." And I cannot recall that the shepherd ever looked back. There, before my eyes was a scene known well to Jesus' hearers: "I am the good shepherd. I know my own sheep and my own know me. My sheep know my voice. A stranger's voice they will not follow" (John 10). At the call of the shepherd's voice, the sheep were sorting themselves—and following.

Basic in the New Testament understanding of Christ the Good Shepherd is the concept of belonging to one another. The hired hand is one to whom the sheep do not belong. "The hired hand runs away because he does not care for the sheep" but "I am the good shepherd. . . . And I lay down my life for the sheep" (John 10:13, 15). The shepherd cares and the sheep know it!

Out of the shepherd's "knowing" and "caring" comes "knowing" and "trust" from the sheep. At the end of the day those sheep knew and followed the voice of their shepherd. They had learned over the years that there would be water and perhaps more food. At the close of that day they would be gathered in a corral safe from thieves and wild animals, with the shepherd's own body on the ground, the gate of the sheepfold!

Though most Americans have never seen a shepherd tending a flock of sheep, we are told over and again that the image of the good shepherd is the best known and most widely loved of all the New Testament images. Jesus would use this very model in the post-resurrection "rehabilitation/commissioning" of Peter: "Peter, do you love me? Feed/Tend my sheep" (John 21).

Many, if not most, Protestant churches refer to their ministers as "pastors." That's the Latin word for shepherd. Not a few give a strange English twist to that Latin word and speak about "pastoring" congregations.

Our people want to respect their pastors and they do, from the very beginning of a new ministry. But trust is another matter. Trust is a quality that grows in our experiences of respect and trustworthiness. I learned when I was elected bishop that from the announcement of the election I was given the title and respect of the office almost instantly. Learning to trust my judgment and placing the care of pastoral vocations and congregational life in my hands—those were another matter. In their "trusting" our people must experience caring, belonging, and faithfulness. Trust is neither quickly learned nor thoughtlessly given; it requires some serious "living together" in the ministry of the church.

Trust is rarely established in any meaningful depth when folks believe their pastor will be "here today and gone tomorrow." It is not built very successfully when congregants believe that their pastor sees them and the parish as a "stepping stone" to something better, bigger, richer, or more challenging. I am convinced that such "pastors" can hardly feel like anything other than a "hireling" to these parishes, no matter his or her skills or informed organizational systems. At least at the beginning, I am firmly convinced that when a new pastor begins, there must be a sense that this shepherd is entering into this ministry with them "for the long haul." Later experiences may suggest otherwise, but every beginning must demonstrate a sensitive caring for and investment with one another, both pastor and people.

Some years ago, in a metropolitan area of Pennsylvania of about 250,000 people, there were 27 Lutheran congregations. Of these only about five had prospered, were currently strong, and had a depth both of solid lay leadership and financial reserves and resources. A judicatory study was done to determine what made the five different from the 22 other struggling congregations. It was discovered that all five had one thing in common. All had a history of long and stable pastorates. I think that is no accident.

It takes time to build a shared sense of caring that oversteps and grows beyond the power struggles about which we hear so much these days. Pastor Glenn E. Ludwig, himself a pastor serving "for the long haul" in his call, writes well about the importance of long-term pastorates (chapter 2), the importance of the early year(s) (chapter 3), and building trust (chapter 4).

Once trust is built, teaching is more focused and more effective. Leadership is identified and develops quite naturally out of the relations of pastoral leadership and caring. In chapter 7, he deals creatively with styles of leadership, supervision, and development of lay leaders who share vision and lead with enthusiasm.

These are timely topics. One of America's major Protestant denominations has reported that the average pastorate is now about five years. My experience suggests that, in a good pastoral setting and relationship, a five-year pastorate should be at its prime. As we talk with congregational search committees, we speak of and hope/plan for the potential of 10 years in a new pastorate, unless there are known pathologies that require some remedial work and planning. Whether one's definition of a long-term pastorate, one "in it for the long haul," is seven years, 10 years, or even more, there is every reason to believe that the long-term pastorate is more effective for our congregations and more fulfilling for our pastors. This matter of pastors being nurtured and fulfilled in long-term pastorates is essential. The same denomination lamenting the current five-year average for pastorates now recommends that congregations provide sabbatical times on a five-year rotation, providing for and encouraging continuing education, intentional self-care, and appropriate professional disciplines that avoid pastoral burnout. The hope is that the five-year sabbatical rotation will both better equip those who serve and extend the pastorates as well.

Recently a pastor called me, asking to preach the ordination sermon for a member of his congregation. His sermon spoke of the ordinand's "splash" in the baptismal font on the day of his baptism. After the liturgy I said, "Pastor, you have been here a long time." "Twenty-eight years!" he responded with enthusiasm and a broad smile. "I married his parents, I baptized him and his brothers and sisters. I confirmed him, and today I preached at his ordination. This congregation started me out in ministry and it is still exciting." A rather new building and nave, a couple of fine choirs, and a sea of smiling people who knew and liked each other told me in a moment why it was still exciting.

To quote Pastor Ludwig: "At the end of our analysis, the bottom line of it all is really the one advantage that outlasts, outweighs, and outshines all the disadvantages—long-term pastorates tend to lead to healthier congregations" (p. 16).

This is a timely book both for pastors beginning in new ministries as well as those who seek to debrief and untangle issues in ongoing ministries. Well-researched and organized, it is written by a pastor who continues to serve "for the long haul" in his congregation in a continuing and exciting ministry, a pastor who continues to live out the call of the good shepherd:

"He calls his own sheep by name and leads them out. When he has brought out all his own, he goes ahead of them and the sheep follow him because they know his voice" (John 10:3b-5).

THE REV. DR. THEODORE F. SCHNEIDER, BISHOP
Metropolitan Washington D.C. Synod
Evangelical Lutheran Church in America

ACKNOWLEDGMENTS

Of all the books I have written, this one was by far the most collaborative effort of them all. Therefore, I owe a debt of gratitude to many people who were part of the effort, ideas, and completion of this project.

First of all, a number of folks at the Alban Institute need to be thanked. Roy Oswald would, of course, be the first. His seminar on "New Visions for the Long Pastorate" provided the basis for my reflections on this issue and much of the research behind the reflections. Thanks to Richard Bass and Claudia Greer for putting together the resource list at the end of the book. Finally, I need to say a word of deep appreciation to David Lott, managing editor. It was he who encouraged the writing of this book, and who shepherded this writer through the entire process. His knowledge, his gift for critical review, and his ever-availability were invaluable to me. I value his insights and ideas and am grateful for this opportunity to have worked with this highly respected organization.

Second, I need to say a word or two of thanks to the people who, 17 years ago, called a young chaplain to be their pastor. The staff of First Lutheran Church in Ellicott City, Maryland, has been most supportive and helpful in the writing of this book. They were understanding of my constant stewing about this project and offered their prayers and support. The congregation council also needs to be mentioned. The leadership of the church has always encouraged my writing, and this project was no exception. I appreciated especially the writing sabbatical time given at critical times in the project. Finally, the members of First Lutheran also deserve honorable mention here. First Lutheran Church is a high-demand, high-expectation, and high-challenge congregation that pulls the best out of me regularly. It expects quality ministry and looks for leadership among its staff. The ministry we have shared together fills the pages of this book and I continue to feel called to serve in this marvelous place.

There are two others who should be mentioned here that deserve my thanks and appreciation. Lyle Schaller, church consultant and prolific writer, was the first to encourage my writing. He gave me that opportunity almost 30 years ago in his "Creative Leadership Series." That chance to express myself through written word launched what has been an important part of my ministry ever since. I am forever grateful for his keen instincts, his friendship, and his prodding to express myself clearly and creatively.

Finally, there is someone who has always been here for and with me: Stella, wife and advisor, has stood by my side through all the valleys and mountains of this journey of ministry together. Her love and support have given me strength for the long haul and it is to her that I dedicate this book.

CHAPTER 1

Confessions–Absolution–Grace
Where It All Should Begin

He is young and not long from his seminary days. It is his second parish and he has served there long enough to understand now what he faces. And he is hurting.

It is an all-too-familiar scenario. A bright young pastor comes to serve an established church and faces unforeseen obstacles early on in his ministry. However, this story (a true one, sadly) has another subplot that multiplies the seriousness of the struggle this young man faces. He has been called to serve a congregation that has recently said goodbye to a pastor they've known and loved for 32 years.

Those of us on the sidelines of this struggle—that is, those of us in neighboring parishes—knew that this was going to be a difficult situation for anyone stepping into impossible shoes to fill. We just didn't know when the shadow would begin to fall.

During a recent pastor's meeting the young man began to share the pain. And it was then that one of our colleagues gave some very interesting and sage advice to the young pastor: "Consider yourself an interim, until otherwise notified."

The truth in that statement sounded very familiar to my own experience and I've ruminated on it for some time.

My Journey–A Confession (of Sorts)

You see, the university was a great place to be. I was enjoying my role as chaplain and teacher to young people. I was established, respected, and having fun.

Then the phone call came from my bishop. He asked me to do him a favor. Now, one doesn't approach such requests lightheartedly. How often does a bishop ask for a favor? He wanted me to interview at a parish in another state. He told me they were ready to make a decision on a candidate, but they wanted to interview someone from outside their immediate area so they could get some perspective. The bishop thought I could give them a decent interview and help them articulate their challenges.

In the initial interview, I heard some of the history. This parish had enjoyed a series of senior pastors—all seemingly gifted and beloved persons. In fact, since 1922 the parish had only had three senior pastors, with pastorates of 22, 27, and 11 years consecutively. Now they were looking for new pastor to give leadership for a major building project.

What began as a favor turned into a call to ministry. And I wish the wise colleague who had said to the young man in the opening story—"Consider yourself an interim, until otherwise notified"—had been around to advise me as well.

The Interim: More Confessions

For two-and-a-half years I struggled to "pay my dues" (more on what that means later). The initial stages of any call to serve begin with excitement. But, in my case, that excitement soon gave way to incredulity. I believed God had called me to this parish. I believed that God had gifted me with tools necessary to serve in this setting. I trusted those gifts and my God to see me through. But nothing worked—not my best efforts at preaching and worship leadership; not my organizational, administrative, or time management skills; not even my personality, which has never gotten in my way before. Nothing worked! It was the most difficult time in my entire ministerial life.

Within months I feared I was an unintentional interim who had left a wonderful ministry to respond to what I thought at the time was a new call to serve. But alas and forsooth, maybe I was called to clear the way for someone else, to act as a guide through a transition period, and to set the stage for the main actor yet to come (pick any metaphor you like there).

My incredulity gave way to German stubbornness. I was bound and determined to make a go of it. But even that wasn't enough.

What literally kept me alive in this interim was worship. That is where I felt nurtured. The community that gathered in worship was not the same community that fought my every idea. This faith community gathered around God's Word and the sacraments was a blessed body of seekers, sojourners, believers, and I was one of them. It was in worship that my call felt most affirmed and my gifts for preaching and teaching began to be seen, appreciated, and welcomed.

Then, something happened that changed my interim ministry into a full call—I had a heart attack at the age of 41 (I do not recommend this, by the way, as a way to make that change). However, the response of the congregation notified me of a change in my status: I was now their pastor. People began to express their love and concern for my wife and me. The governing board of the church rallied around me, assuring me that they would handle the details of ministry while I recuperated. And, perhaps the most telling of all for a Lutheran parish, they sent food—lots and lots of casseroles, a sure sign of acceptance and caring.

We still had a long way to go, but the corner had been turned. My unintentional interim, where I feared I might just serve a few years and prepare the congregation for change, had become the call I thought I had accepted back in 1985.

The heart attack was the watershed mark for acceptance, but the groundwork had been laid in worship and pastoral care, where people began to know me not as the "new" pastor, but as their pastor in a time of need.

Sixteen years later, this is still an exciting call where I continue to rely on God's grace everyday. Worship is still the heartbeat of our existence, but now it is not so much a place to prove myself, as it is a place for God to speak to us of community, forgiveness, reconciliation, and truth.

There But For the Grace of God Go . . .

In this book I intend to share some of the learnings and insights from this journey, which hopefully will help to answer some key questions: What has 16 years taught me about long-term pastorates? What about the wisdom of others? What do their voices tell us about their journeys and what can we learn from one another? And what about our congregations? How can they prepare themselves for long-term ministries?

It is an exciting time to be the church, I think. As I write this we are still coping with the events of September 11, 2001. I probably don't even have to say what those events are; the day is etched into our psyches forever. In the days and weeks that followed, our churches were packed with people looking for answers, and if not answers, comfort and support. Our people trust us with their bruised and battered selves and we have a particular word to speak of God to them. The flag will be raised and sung to all across this country of ours, but it is in the churches where God's Word will be spoken—a Word of comfort and challenge.

I have been grateful for the privilege of speaking God's Word during this difficult time. I am also grateful for the years I have walked together with the good people of this parish. Many have called to thank me for my years of service, even though it is not an anniversary year, because they have looked to the church for stability and hope. We who speak God's Word can offer that for the long haul.

Maybe a word or two about my background will ground this discussion for everyone. I come from a confessional faith tradition, one that is rich in liturgy, strong in doctrine, and committed to education. The process by which our church gets a pastor is a call process, not an appointment system. The congregations, with advice and counsel from the Office of the Bishop, call a pastor to serve, normally without limits of time. The pastor and the congregation can stay wedded as long as they mutually choose to do so.

Several years ago, after being "notified" that I was no longer an interim pastor and anticipating the opportunity to serve for many years, I attended the Alban Institute conference on long-term pastorates. Almost 10 years later, I have found the insights, information, and learnings shared in that conference to have been validated in my own call and experience.

So, what I hope to do in this book is to share those learnings from the perspective of one who has "been" there, who has lived through the insights, and who has garnered some of his own. Am I an expert? Certainly not! I am simply one who lives in the trenches of parish life and cares deeply about ministry.

Well, the prelude is about over. It has, hopefully, prepared us for what is to come. We have made a good confession and the absolution has reminded us all of the Rock upon which we all stand. The brief autobiographical history could be recited with "Amazing Grace" being sung in the background—it provides a perspective for forging ahead.

Now we say "Amen," and move first to what we've all heard at one time or another about being in one place for "too" long. Let's call them "myths and legends" and see how many you've heard, maybe believed, and found simply not to be true in the long haul of things.

CHAPTER 2

Myths and Legends
What We've All Heard . . . and Maybe Believe

Before we tackle the issue of the myths we've heard about the effectiveness of long-term pastorates, we should probably take a moment or two to define the phrase itself. We need a point of reference for our discussion together. What, after all, do we mean by long-term pastorates? For instance, do we use as a point of measure the number of sermons preached? Or, how about the number of meetings attended? There are certainly enough pastors attending enough meetings that a case could be made for fulfilling some kind of God-ordained quota of meetings and thereby earning the right to call oneself "long term." How about persons visited as the measure? Or maybe hair loss or weight gain?

What measure do we use so we are all on the same playing field as we move into the issues surrounding the topic of this book? Well, let me suggest seven years as the break point. When a pastor has served for seven years or more, we shall consider that long-term in that setting.

Why Seven Years?

Let me admit right from the start that there is no hard and fast line of demarcation as to when a pastor can consider him- or herself a long-term pastor. Part of the determination has to do with the mindset of the pastor. Are we in it for the long haul? Do we see ourselves staying where we feel God has called us for enough time to accomplish what we believe God has called us to do in our setting? Do we regularly engage in a deliberate discernment process to assess our call? Do we continue to feel and know that this is where God wishes for us to serve?

This is not meant to sound overly pious. We must begin at the point of assessment of the call. Did we take this call with any spoken or unspoken assumptions about how long we intended to serve? If we are in a first call situation, the likelihood of staying for our entire ministerial life is, indeed, very slim. But if we have served for some time and have the experience to serve in a challenging setting, do we look upon that call as one that will be of a duration that is beyond the get-acquainted stage with the congregation?

These are real questions we have to ask ourselves and assess the answers. Part of what makes a long-term pastorate long-term is the intentionality of the pastor and that person's discernment of God's call for him or her to serve in that particular place. As William Willimon has written in his insightful book on the ordained life, "Vocation to service, in my opinion, is one of the main sources of motivation for constancy in ministry."[1] Although he was talking about the character of the clergyperson, his reference to constancy is appropriate for our discussion here.

We need to add here, also, that there are times when our calls must be reissued, if you will; times when we will need to reassess our call to serve in a particular setting to discover what God has in mind for us and for those who called us. For instance, a few years ago the church where I serve finished a major building program. It was a project for which I had been called to give leadership. Upon completing the building program after 11 years, however, I had the sense that I needed to have my call to serve here reaffirmed. Maybe my work was completed and it was up to someone else to take the congregation through its next steps. Maybe my gifts for ministry, of organization, process, and leadership, were not what the congregation now needed as it faced the question, "Who are we now that the new building is done?" Eleven years is a long time to wrap oneself around a project. The project itself becomes a major part of how you define yourself. And, once it is completed, there is a need not only to celebrate the accomplishment but also to ask, "What next?" Any pastor who has been involved in such a major project knows the truth of this example. It is not insignificant that about 80 percent of pastors who are involved in building projects leave within two years of completion of the project. Why? Some would say that they used all their ministerial "currency" to complete the work. That can certainly be the case. But a significant factor in the leaving has to do with discernment of call and gifts, not only by the pastor but also by the served congregation.

So, discernment of call is an ongoing process that can, even if one does not begin with the assumptions of long-term ministry, lead one to stay in a call beyond the initial stages and even the completion of a major project, and find it challenging, rewarding, and blessed.

But back to the question of "Why seven years?" In discussing this topic for many years with clergy of different denominations, it is the consensus that something happens in a pastorate between five and seven years of service. Certainly the evidence is anecdotal, but worthy of reflection nonetheless.

I repeat: Something happens in a pastorate somewhere between five and seven years. There is movement. Decisions seem to come in an easier rhythm. The interchange of ideas and the ability to dialogue in open and honest fashion seems to increase. In short, there is a change in the relationship between pastor and people. The trust that has taken time to develop has laid the groundwork for growth, depth, and change to arise from a foundation of respect and love.

Let me interject another story from my experience to illustrate. I was called, as I mentioned before, to give leadership to a major building program. When I arrived here I discovered that the congregation intended to tackle this building project in two phases. The first phase was to set the stage for the main part of the project, namely a new worship space. As I talked to architects and builders, as well as to other clergy who have survived building programs, it became obvious to me that we could save a good deal of money and experience less interruption to our ministry if we did everything at once and not in two steps. It was a plan that made sense. It was the right thing to do by all standards of measurement. It was, indeed, good stewardship of time and resources, for it would save money in the long run and concentrate all our efforts at one time. It was the right thing to do for all the right reasons.

Except . . . except it was bad timing. I had not been here long enough for this congregation to trust me. The relationship with the leadership hadn't developed to the point where new ideas could be entertained because trust had not developed in our working relationship together. Therefore, my good, right, stewardship-based idea was soundly rejected. It wasn't a matter of people wanting to put this new pastor in his place (I had only been here a little over two years at the time of the meeting and vote). It was a matter of not being trusted.

So, the something that happens between a pastor and a congregation, beginning with the leadership with whom a pastor works, that something that occurs between five and seven years is trust. We will examine this important concept of trust development in a later chapter.

After seven years of faithful, dedicated, and consistent ministry, noticeable things begin to happen. By now, the pitch and tone of the congregation has been influenced by the pastor's style. The leadership of the church should begin to reflect the priorities and passions of a working relationship with the pastor. A style of leadership has been imprinted. The "dues" have been paid (more on that later, also).

So, for purposes of our discussion together, let's assume the high-end number of seven years as a working definition. Are there times when one "arrives" before that? Certainly. Are there times when it may take longer to feel and be established? Probably. But let's take the seven-year mark as the number so we have common ground: Long-term pastorates are hereby declared to be seven years and counting.

The Voices We've Heard . . . and Maybe Believe

There have always been those voices around that share a common refrain: "Long-term pastorates are unhealthy for the church." Each of those voiced concerns holds a degree of truth, and in some situations those voices have been absolutely on the money.

But that does not mean that long-term pastorates are by their very nature bad for the church. Yes, each of the voices we are about to hear raise legitimate concerns. We shall acknowledge those issues forthrightly, but I, for one, won't be led to join in the expected refrain. Instead, as each voice is raised, we shall hear a different chorus offered as antagonist.

"The church goes stale."

This should probably be the last of the voices because it is the melody line for all the other voices we shall hear. But because it is the melody and most of us have heard it a time or two, we need to hear it in simple plain song and not move too quickly to the conclusive refrain we know tags along.

Is it possible for a church that has had a pastor for a long time to go stale? Absolutely. It is a known and familiar melody. But a few questions which challenge the assumption that it is the long-term pastorate which causes this staleness keep us from running willy-nilly toward the assumed refrain.

Is it the long-term pastor who causes the church to go stale? If yes, to what degree? If the church is, indeed, lay- and clergy-led, what about the responsibility of the laity to keep staleness from occurring? What is the role of the laity in defining the mission and informing the vision for God's people? Furthermore, can't a short-term pastorate become just as stale?

You see, the freshness for ministry is not about length of service. To be sure, ruts can develop on any well-traveled road (to add another metaphor). But sameness, routine, ruttedness can occur in any relationship when people don't pay attention to what God's fresh voice is calling them to be and do. The church going stale is a function of loss of energy and focus, so that we continue to sit in the same wagon, going down the same road, while singing the same melody and not going anywhere in particular.

Freshness, vitality, energy, and leadership are certainly part of the pastor's responsibility. If we are not excited about ministry and serving God in the setting where we have been called, how can we expect others to be excited? Whether we want to accept it or not, the reality is that the pastor sets the tone for ministry. But the called leadership of the parish also has responsibility here. If the ministry gets into a rut, the programs lose interested participants, and the energy for service has diminished, it is not entirely the fault of the pastor and/or the paid staff.

This melody line can serve as a wake-up call to reexamine ministry and to ask where God is calling a congregation to move. It does not have to lead to the refrain, "Therefore, our long-term pastorate is unhealthy!"

"Everyone gets too comfortable."

This voice is sung along with the melody line, often as harmony to it. And there is the same degree of truth as in the melody above it.

As before, we need to ask whether "getting too comfortable" is an effect caused by a long-term pastorate, or are there other contributors? And, as before, we need to point to the leadership, both paid and volunteer. (An aside here for a moment. I like to use the word *server* rather than *volunteer* when referring to those who give of their time and talents in the church. We do not volunteer in church; we live out our baptismal calling in the community as servants one of another.)

The danger with a church getting too comfortable is that we lose our sense of mission. We become a club whose purpose is to serve its members and have them feel good, rather than to be a servant community who is challenged by God's Word and Spirit. Maybe we should just take the "too" from the harmony line and acknowledge that being comfortable is never a goal for God's people.

"The pastor begins to coast."

We move to the bass clef and take up the harmony from the ranks of the ordained. In a long-term pastorate, it is indeed true a pastor can begin to coast, especially if he or she is facing a few years of ministry before retirement and feels stuck in a current call. That stuckness can be the result of economic necessities like a spouse's profession and income, or the salary level a pastor has attained and the fear that another pastoral setting could not match it. The stuckness could also be the result of age. Like it or not, there is a churchly bias about age of clergy. Ask anyone seeking a call after he or she turns 55. It's difficult after a certain age, salary, and experience level to move and a pastor can easily settle in and coast rather than risk the battle to change.

"It's easy for the pastor to 'go native.'"

This bass clef has other harmonies that flow from the one just mentioned; the fear of the pastor "going native" is one of them. "Going native" means to become so assimilated into the culture and lifestyle of the parish that one loses the ability to be prophetic, to stand to the side of one's setting, and to pronounce God's Word of comfort and challenge. When a pastor "goes native," the ability even to see issues clearly is compromised. We develop the fear of speaking the truth because doing so could push us out of the tent where we've worked hard to fit in.

The refrain of "long-term pastorates are unhealthy" could be sung if this bass clef is the dominant theme of a pastor's ministry. But, as with the treble clef mentioned earlier, it does not have to be that way. There is a degree of vigilant attention to God's Spirit needed in all ministries. The long-term pastor does not automatically go stale after X number of years just as the pastor of a long-term call does not always get inducted into the native culture's inner circle. There are measures one can take that can keep both from happening (chapter 5 addresses both of those in detail).

"The pastor becomes too powerful."

There is a bass line to the tune we've been dealing with in this chapter. A bass line often gives substance to a song. It provides a grounding, a footing, or a base (excuse the pun) on which the rest of the music stands. This bass line is no exception.

A pastor can become very powerful over time in a congregation; there is no denying that. It is a fact and a reality. However, whether the pastor becomes too powerful, whether the bass line becomes too dominant, is more a function of the personality of the pastor and the relationship with the elected leadership of the church. Is the leadership able and willing to challenge the pastor over issues of ministry? And can that challenge be done in a way that is mutually upbuilding for the pastor, the leadership, and the church? Not all challenges need to take on a confrontational tone.

Ministry needs to be collegial at many levels—among staff, between elected leaders and pastor/staff, and within the broader body of the church. Power in a congregation should come only from God's Spirit, which empowers all of us; that is not a matter of years served, but a matter of prayer and discernment by the whole community of faith.

External Influences on Long-Term Pastorates

There are several external factors that can certainly affect long-term pastorates. These influences are fairly new to the scene. To be sure, the influence of these external factors does not automatically translate into an effective ministry. Any or all of these factors could actually contribute to a pastor "going native" or to a pastor staying in a call that has gone stale. However, each of these factors influences whether a pastor will stay in a situation for the long haul. Whether that staying is healthy for the pastor and/or the congregation is another matter. Suffice it to say that these external factors can have bearing on how long a pastor chooses to stay in a particular ministry setting.

Home Ownership vs. Parsonage

Over the last 20 years there has been a decided trend away from congregations providing parsonages to pastors. Instead, congregations increasingly are offering pastors a housing allowance to encourage home ownership. The advantages to home ownership are numerous and obvious, with the building up of equity being the major one.

It is certainly not easy just to pick up and move when a capital investment like a home is involved. It is easy to move from parsonage to parsonage, but selling a home and then buying another is a big investment of time and energy. It would seem that owning a home would make it more desirable for a pastor to stay in one place longer; after all, even home equity takes time to accumulate. Then there is the message such home ownership sends to the members of the church: It says that the pastor is willing to invest in that community, and hopefully, in their community of faith.

I can think of at least one caveat to this point about parsonages making it easier for a pastor to move: Some congregations that have a parsonage for the pastor and his or her family to live in also offer an equity allowance so that the pastor can not only build up some resources, but also may, some day, own a home either in that community or close by. It goes without saying that it is harder to move when property is involved. I entertained a move several years ago that would have placed my wife and I over halfway across this land. One of the major factors that lead me to withdraw my name was that we owned a beach house, bought with an equity allowance. We simply could not see ourselves giving that up and moving a major distance away.

The Spouse's Profession, Calling, and Employment

We live in a time when most American homes have two working incomes. That truism applies to pastoral homes as well. More clergy spouses than ever work outside of the home, many with professional careers that are important to them. They, too, have received a call to serve in a vocation and setting, and their gifts for service and their calls must be honored as well.

The ability to transfer locations when multiple professional careers are at stake is an issue for pastoral families these days. Not all jobs and vocations are easily transferable. For instance, there was a time when a spouse who was a teacher could easily move locations, find another teaching assignment, and be gainfully and, hopefully, happily employed. The pendulum of that profession currently has swung to the other end. Now, if a teacher has more than 10 years experience, many school systems will not even interview them for a position because they can get a person with less experience with less money. The general rule of thumb has become the longer one is in a profession, the harder it is to move locations and find a suitable position that pays according to one's experience level.

Because the covenant of marriage is a binding covenant, and within that covenant there needs to be mutual respect and support, the professional life of a pastor's spouse needs to be considered when a pastoral move is being contemplated. This works the other way as well, when the spouse receives a career opportunity that may cause a need to relocate. Then, the pastor becomes the one seeking another call.

The Ages and Life Situations of Children

There has always been a discussion among parents about when is the right and wrong time to move children into different schools. The same situation applies to clergy who have school-age children. Certainly children adjust fairly easily to new situations, but there are ages and situations in which those moves are more difficult.

For instance, it would be difficult to explain to a high school junior that next year, their senior year, they would be in a different school because his or her family, the pastor's family, is moving to another town or state. There are those students who would welcome such a move, but the majority would find it difficult and maybe painful to leave classmates, friends, and a known school environment.

If the student is in college, however, he or she is already moving beyond the sphere of home and community to establish his or her own life. A pastoral move while a student is in college is much less difficult than if the student is still in high school.

Let's push the calendar up a few years and picture a pastor with grown children, off on their own, with children of their own. Now grandchildren enter into the picture. Being a grandfather is the most rewarding profession I have ever encountered. When new grandparents in my parishes used to regale me with stories of the wonders of their super grandkids, complete with pictures of Halloween costumes or funny faces, I would be polite, but wonder about the sanity level of those people. Now, I proudly count myself among them! And the thought of moving, or relocating, far from those grandkids is not even in my imagination.

So, the ages and life-situations of the children (and grandchildren) come into play with long-term pastorates. It is kind of an unspoken rule that one should not relocate while children are in high school. Before high school, yes. After high school, yes. But the importance of family ties cannot be easily dismissed even after the children are out on their own.

Congregational Culture

Congregations have histories. They also have cultures and mindsets and expectations of their clergy. What is the pattern and history of the pastorate that is being served or one that is calling a pastor? Has it had a history of short-term pastorates? Does it see itself as a training ground for pastors right out of seminary who will be with them four to six years and then move on? Has the congregation had long-term pastorates in its history and what has been their judgment about that experience? Was it remembered as a good thing or a bad thing?

One of the realities a pastor must face is that it is often hard to follow a long-term pastorate. The congregation may say they want the next pastor to be another long-term pastor, but the transition from a long-term pastor to any other pastor is often difficult. The new pastor might find him- or herself as an unintentional interim who will bridge the gap between what was and what can be for the future.

How a congregation sees itself and this call they are offering a pastor is critical to whether this will become a long-term pastorate or not. Are they looking for leadership for the long haul? Is there a major program or project for which they need specific leadership that will take some time and effort on behalf of a leader-pastor? Is there enough challenge here so that the pastor and the people can grow together, changing as circumstances dictate, and always being responsive to God's leading and guiding? Are the skills, gifts, and talents of the pastor adaptable as a congregation and its ministry changes over time?

One of the downsides of long-term pastorates has been that the congregation itself may take advantage of the pastor. One often makes a financial sacrifice for staying in one place for a long time. I know that I have made some sacrifices for the sake of the ministry here, especially while beginning a major building program and dealing with the risks of financial deficits. Although I have been fortunate to serve a congregation that was able to move forward in its support of staff, many congregations have not been able to do so, with the result that pastors and their families have consistently had to make financial sacrifices.

Mobility Issues in the Denomination

There is one final external factor that must be considered—mobility. How easy or hard is it to move in a particular denominational system? In an appointment system, that all depends on the one doing the appointment, but in an open call system, other factors surround the ease of mobility.

One must first examine the cycle of surplus and deficit among pastors. Are there more pastors wanting to move than there are churches available? Is the denomination facing a surplus of pastors and therefore having difficulty finding viable calls for clergy? Obviously, in surplus years it is harder to move and relocate. Denominational differences do come into play here, but the law of supply and demand does as well.

Another factor affecting mobility is the role of the judicatory in the process. Many judicatories are taking more seriously their role in matching candidates for calls with ministry opportunities. A good match of candidate gifts and personality can lead to a viable, energetic, and effective long-term pastorate. Not only will a bad match fail to achieve such a goal, but it can affect the future ministries of the candidate and the congregation as well. This issue needs someone with judicatory experience to explicate further, but let us just note that judicatories are seeing the results of their efforts and noting that there are long-term effects, both positive and negative.

Key Research Findings

In the late 1970s and early 1980s, the Alban Institute set out to research the effect of long-term pastorates on congregations and pastors. Their research findings were published in 1983 in a monograph, *New Visions for the Long Pastorate*. This book and the research became the impetus for the seminars that Alban has held on the topic.

In their research, six main advantages to what they termed "long-tenured pastorates" were identified. The data actually reversed the previous negative assumptions that were held by the researchers and verified the possibility of healthy, growing long-tenured pastorates for both clergy and congregations. The six advantages they identified were:

1. A long-tenured pastorate makes possible greater in-depth knowledge of and relationships between the pastor and individual church members as well as between clergy and the congregation as a whole;

2. Experiencing a long-tenured pastorate makes possible cumulative developing knowledge and experience of each other for both clergy and congregation, as they observe and participate in each other's growth over time;

3. Greater continuity and stability of leadership and program in a long-tenured pastorate makes possible events not possible during a short tenure;

4. A long-tenured pastorate opens up possibilities of greater personal and spiritual growth for both clergy and congregation;

5. A long-tenured pastorate makes possible deeper knowledge of and participation by the clergy in the community (local, professional, ecumenical, larger denominational); and

6. A long-tenured pastorate allows additional personal benefits for both the clergy and his/her family.[2]

The Advantage That Outweighs All the Disadvantages

We are at the bottom line, finally. Now we need to tally up the positives and negatives. There are clearly plenty of both and, like in all areas of life, a positive can easily become a negative (and vice versa).

At the end of our analysis, the bottom line of it all is really the one advantage that outlasts, outweighs, and outshines all the disadvantages—long-term pastorates tend to lead to healthier congregations.

How do we know this? Three sources give us the confidence to proclaim that, if not as fact, then as an observable hypothesis. First, the Alban Institute makes this claim in its seminars on long-term pastorates.

The basis for their claim comes from their consultations, research, and experience in working with parishes and pastors. Second, judicatory officials tend to make the same pronouncement. Many have observed it as true in their jurisdictions. Finally, I invite the reader to look around and reflect on the parishes and pastors you have known who have been in long-term situations. As I have done that, I see, time after time, congregations who are viable, healthy, and growing.

What are the signs of that health? Many have written on that subject, but a list would include, but not be limited to, the following:

- sense of mission
- stronger outreach into the community
- growth in stewardship over the years
- active participation by its members
- a sense that things are happening in fresh and creative ways

All are signs of health and the long-term pastor is a major player in that arena.

❖   ❖   ❖

It is time to turn our attention back to the beginning, the beginning of that critical relationship between a pastor and a congregation. How we begin, what foot we start on, has much to do with how and when the "Amen" is pronounced at the end of that relationship. So, let's push backward and examine those critical first years of ministry.

CHAPTER 3

Honeymoon vs. Trial

Surviving the Critical First Years

The first years in any profession can be critical years. It is the time when one develops professional identity. It is a time of learning what one was not taught in any academic school about the profession. It is a time of developing working models that can carry one through an entire career. Beginning that profession in a positive, constructive, healthy, and creative way is, therefore, crucial.

The ministry is no exception to this hypothesis. Whether this is a first call or a fourth call to serve, how one begins can set the tone for later years. We have all known clergy who began badly, for a myriad of reasons, and never recovered from that beginning. The likelihood of a pastorate becoming long term can be somewhat determined by how the ministry in that setting began. Those critical first years must be navigated with wisdom, maturity, and integrity.

The Old Myth

Many have been around long enough to have heard the old myth about beginning a pastorate. The conventional wisdom, seemingly passed down through seminaries and word of mouth, went something like this: The beginning of a relationship between a pastor and a congregation is the "honeymoon period." Remember that?

It was taught, or at least assumed, that the start of any ministerial relationship had many of the same qualities of that period we call a honeymoon—that time right after a man and woman join in marriage. Although this period could be brief, it was nevertheless thought that the longer one could maintain that honeymoon feeling, the better off one was.

Many of the same characteristics of a couple enjoying that beginning stage of marriage also seemed to describe the beginning of a pastorate. First, there is *the getting-to-know-you part*. We think we know the person whom we are marrying, but soon discover there are things about which we were clueless. The beginning of a pastoral relationship is much the same. We are learning about one another and, in a congregational setting, that can take some time.

Second, the beginning of a marriage relationship is characterized as *a time of idealism*. He married a beautiful Queen; she married the charming Prince. In a congregational setting, the congregation might feel that they have called their "perfect" pastor, and the pastor feels that this is the "perfect" place for him or her. It is a wonderful feeling, to be sure. Not very realistic, but wonderful.

The period of idealism will ultimately give way in a marriage to some reality. She isn't the ideal he had envisioned and he is really something less than what she had bargained for. Realism, however discouraging, takes the place of idealism.

The same is true in a pastoral relationship. The pastor begins to see that this "perfect" call comes with some imperfections and the congregation begins to notice that the pastor is not the ideal pastor they had wanted.

Third, a honeymoon period is *exciting*. Everything is new and fresh. Some have said that being "in love" can affect our senses. Our sense of smell is heightened, as is our sense of color. There have been studies showing that in this stage of relationship, our bodies produce a chemical response caused by the other person.

Now, this physiological change has never been proven to be the case with a pastor and congregation, but there is something of the same kind of excitement about a new call. Everything is fresh. All the human encounters are new and ripe with possibilities. There is no history to repeat, forgive, or overcome. The future is open and exciting. It is, all in all, a wonderful place to be.

Two Basic Approaches Advocated in the Myth

The myth has given birth to two very different approaches as to how one handles this honeymoon period in a pastorate. In fact, the approaches are so different as to be polar opposites of one another.

The first approach to the supposed honeymoon period advocates that the pastor should make all the changes he or she can during this time. The philosophy behind this approach tells us that since the congregation "loves" the pastor so much, make changes before the "in love-ness" fades. For instance, if the pastor wants to change something in the worship service, now is a good time. The congregation will be more accepting of the change and will likely go along with it. If the pastor wants to change a program, or add a program that otherwise has not been done, now is a good time. The congregation will be more open to new ideas in the honeymoon period and the pastor should strike while the iron is hot. If the pastor wants to move to a different form of administrative management, now is the time, according to proponents of this approach. The congregation believes that the pastor is the ideal person for them and will more openly embrace such a change. The examples are endless, but the philosophy is the same—make as many changes as you want and can during this time period. You may not get this chance again.

The second approach stands opposite to the one just espoused—make few if any changes during the honeymoon period. The working philosophy behind this approach advocates that we should not use up all our pastoral currency during the initial stages of ministry; we may need some for later. This approach calls for a period of listening and learning about the parish and its people. One needs to learn something of the particular setting of the congregation, including the culture and norms of operation. A pastor needs to develop relationships so that future decisions can be made in a spirit of dialogue and mutuality. It is important to "pay your dues," so to speak—get to know the people, offer faithful service, and build upon relationships so that ministry can flourish collegially rather then by pastoral fiat.

The wisdom of both of these approaches assumes that there is a honeymoon period at the beginning of a pastor's relationship with a congregation and her people. But what if, in reality, that honeymoon period does not exist?

As I listen to pastors and have observed ministry for almost three decades, I would contend that the honeymoon period is a thing of the past. It may have existed at one time in North American pastorates, but it seems to me that today people are more realistic, if not skeptical, of those in authority, be it a pastor, a principal, or the local police. A cultural mindset seems to have developed that does not take authority for granted, and, therefore, expects those in authority positions to earn the respect and trust of those they serve.

Andrew Greeley, writing from a Roman Catholic perspective, weighs in on a personal note with his experience: "I learned very quickly in my first assignment that respect was no longer given, save in a superficial way. It had to be earned by the display of professional competence. That is all the more true today."[1]

My experience and observations support Greeley's assertions. The honeymoon period, if it ever indeed existed, is a thing of the past. What has replaced it (or, at least, what most pastors experience) is, for lack of better words, a period of trial and testing.

The Reality That Replaces the Myth

Theories abound regarding interpersonal relationships, group dynamics, and group growth. They may differ in terminology, but all of them offer a way to systematize what happens when people come together in one group or another. But even if the terminology differs, they all agree that there is a process with developmental stages for all groups.

One of the clearer versions comes from Richard C. Weber in an article titled "The Group: A Cycle from Birth to Death."[2] Weber claims that all groups proceed through three major stages of development comparable to a person's infant, adolescent, and adult stages. In turn, each stage has four dimensions that need attention: group behavior, group tasks/issues, interpersonal issues, and leadership issues. Here is how those dimensions play out in each of the stages Weber identifies:

	INFANCY	ADOLESCENCE	ADULTHOOD
Group Behavior:	superficial, ambiguous	establish rules	cohesion
Group Tasks:	orientation, membership	power/influence	functioning
Interpersonal Issues:	inclusion	control	affection
Leadership Issues:	dependency	counter-dependency	inter-dependent

As a pastor enters into a new relationship with a congregation, a new group, if you will, has been formed. What Weber's proposal illustrates (as do other process theories) is that there are many dynamics moving through group relationships. What used to be considered a honeymoon period, illustrated by the infancy period of Weber, has either been dramatically shortened or no longer exists for pastors. For a multitude of reasons, the honeymoon seems to end very shortly after the installation.

The reality now seems to be that the first years are, for lack of a better symbol, marked by more of a trial—a proving of oneself to the members of the congregation. Is this pastor who he or she claims to be? Are the skills of our new pastor matched to our needs?

Comparisons often abound with past pastors and, specifically, with the immediate predecessor. Is our new pastor as good a preacher, or as friendly, or as attentive to me as the last pastor (now often raised to near-sainthood), or as good an administrator? I know of one pastor who got himself into trouble because he did not arrive early to church on Sunday mornings to make the coffee for the volunteers who would be coming to help lead worship, as the former pastor always had done.

Most of the time the questions being asked of the pastor never reach the ears of the person who is "on trial." She or he may not even sense the issues but the questions are there, the comparisons are being made, and judgments are being rendered. And all of this seems to come to a head, or at least becomes more obvious to a pastor, in the first crises of one's ministry.

Those First Crises

Whether the crisis be personal (a death or accident), interpersonal (a fight between two organizations in the church or between leaders), or administrative (a budget crisis), how the new pastor handles any one or all of them will be keenly noticed. As muscles of the human body are tested by resistance, now the strength or weakness of the pastor becomes tested and observed. There are two keys to successfully maneuvering through this minefield.

Response vs. Reaction

First, it is important for any leader of any organization to know the difference between *responding* to a stimulus and *reacting* to one. Then, one must be deliberate in responding to the crisis presented.

Reacting is an automatic and often immediate action. When we touch a hot bowl, we do not have to think about pulling our hand away. We just react. It does not require any thought. It is quick, immediate, automatic, and decisive.

Responding, on the other hand, is a thoughtful and deliberate action. When someone makes a hurtful comment to us, our first reaction may be to sling one back. But often that just escalates the rhetoric and makes things worse. A response measures the words by engaging the brain and thought processes before engaging the mouth.

How many of us, simply as human beings relating to others, have said or done things we wish we had not? Remember that old saying about hindsight being 20/20? But as we mature and learn to monitor ourselves in healthy ways, we find ways to keep ourselves from reacting and saying or doing things we will later regret.

In those first critical years of ministry, as a pastor seeks to establish him or herself, crisis will occur. Someone will die in the parish and the pastor needs to respond appropriately to the crisis and the family. A squabble will break out between the property committee and the youth group over the state of the youth room. The finance committee will sound the alarm that the giving level has dropped off and that bills may not be able to be paid this month. The list of potential crises could go on for some pages here.

It is important for the pastor to be perceived, in the midst of such crises, as a thoughtful, deliberate, calming presence. By responding appropriately to each crisis, the pastor goes a long way toward developing relationships based on trust and respect.

Integrity for the Long Haul

Second, it is equally important for the pastor to act at all times with integrity. *Integrity* is one of those concepts that is sometimes difficult to explain and nail down. I have always said it is kind of like rhythm: We recognize it more quickly in its absence that in its presence. Integrity has to do with character, trustworthiness, and maturity.

The dictionary defines *integrity* as: (1) an unimpaired condition: soundness; (2) adherence to a code of moral, artistic, or other values; (3) the quality or state of being complete or undivided. Synonyms for integrity include *honesty* and *unity*.

For a pastor who is in it for the long haul, integrity is a critical condition. Will the pastor follow through on what he promised? Is the pastor as good as her word? Did the pastor honor the confidentiality of what was shared in private prayer at a bedside? Do the pastor's actions match her words? Is there depth to the preaching that lets the congregation know that the pastor believes what is being spoken with sincerity and conviction? Does the pastor look me in the eye as we talk in the narthex? Can the pastor admit when he is wrong?

Without soundness of character, a pastor's credibility is seriously threatened. I would contend that a pastor who lacks integrity will not have the emotional and psychological maturity to survive over the long haul. When lack of integrity is exposed, any trust that had been developed between a pastor and a congregation is seriously threatened. And when trust does not exist, the opportunities for future ministry will be limited.

Getting Started on the Right Foot

So, how does a pastor get started on the right foot? Is there any magical formula to follow? Are there are clear guidelines? What are some of the principles about getting started that apply to any potentially long-term pastorate?

Whole books have been written on this single issue, but there are three, maybe four, important principles for a pastor to keep in mind as he or she begins in a relationship with a congregation that may lead to a long-term ministry.

Being Clear about Goals and Priorities

Starting up any ministry has the potential to overwhelm even the bravest of ministerial souls. There is so much to learn about the history of the parish, about the way the parish operates, about the people one is called to serve, about the cultural setting of the congregation, and about any staff that are already in place, both paid and volunteer. There is also much to assimilate— the tempo of the culture and how that affects the congregation; the congregation's values, spoken and unspoken; how this congregation understands the pastoral office, just to name a few. And then there is much to do—like visiting the sick and hospitalized, organizing for ministry, preparing sermons for a group of people we do not know, getting the office in shape, finding a home or getting the manse or parsonage in order—the list could go on.

All of this can easily lead to a sense of overload for a new pastor in a new setting. One of the ways to lessen the impact of that overload is to set clear initial goals and priorities for ministry. Some have suggested that one should (*a*) keep those first priorities short term, for they will surely change over time, and (*b*) to state them early, especially to the leadership. Obviously, one of the first general goals would be to get to know the people. Under that global goal the pastor might articulate how he or she is going to accomplish that goal. For instance, when I first came to my current call, I stated my early goal of getting to know people, and then I offered ways I intended to do that: visiting in the home in the first month of all the council members and their families; doing a staff retreat early on with both paid and volunteer staff so that we could share visions and dreams and get to know the gifts we all bring to this ministry we share; and setting up Sunday evening coffee-and-dessert meetings in the church not only to get to know people but to listen to their stories, concerns, and joys. These steps helped me to get started on a clear and decisive path in the ministry that would have otherwise been overwhelming in a large congregation.

Sticking to these early goals and priorities for ministry is important. As we all know, it is easy to get sidetracked as the immediate replaces the important. We should keep those early goals in front of us and assess our ministry on a weekly basis to see how what we did matched or did not match those stated goals.

After six months, revise and edit those goals as other goals and priorities become fairly clear. Do this again after one year. Listening to staff, to leaders, and to members early on will help direct a discerning pastor into ministry goals that will speak to the needs and concerns of the people he or she is called to serve.

One final example from my own experience: My first church council (what we called them back then) meeting went until 1:45 A.M. When I got home, I discovered my wife had locked and bolted me out of the parsonage.

It was one of the worst meetings I had ever attended. In our church system, the council president runs the meetings. In this case, the meeting was ripe with dissension and argumentation. The council had the practice of beginning every meeting with what they called "joys and concerns" of the congregation. It was nothing more than an open forum for gripes and complaints, with people getting extremely defensive as areas of their ministry responsibility came under attack. After a half-hour of such attacks, counterattacks, and growing anger and frustration, we were then supposed to do the business of Christian ministry. Ha! Three people left the meeting in anger and frustration before it was over. I soon discovered that over the past six years half of the council resigned every year because the whole experience was unrewarding.

When my wife let me in and I explained to her, "No, we did not go out to get a drink after the meeting," it became clear to me that one of the goals for my early ministry must be to change the way we talked and dealt with one another, both in council meetings and around the church. As I listened to people before services and at meetings, there was a strong undercurrent of griping and complaining. It was a church pitched in a minor key. That had to change if we were ever going to be effective in ministry and be the people of God who learn to live with and love one another.

We lived out that goal in numerous ways: we started each council meeting with scripturally based devotions and personal sharing; I made it clear that I am willing to listen to any concerns people have, but the one who shares the concern must be willing to work with me to fix the problem; and we learned to laugh together in healthy and healing ways. It sounds like a small thing, but it set the tone for future ministry. I dare say that if we had not turned around the tone of this congregation, I am not sure I would be writing this book and talking about long-term pastorates, at least not in this place.

Pastoral Care in Crises

Certainly a pastor never wishes for personal crises among members, but life brings them and when they come, it is a great opportunity to get to know people. Crises become a quick and immediate way to gain access to our members. We have the unique opportunity and privilege to be invited into people's homes, hearts, and lives during times of need—illness, accidents, hospitalizations, death, divorce or separation. It is a chance to imprint on the congregation and its members that we are caring, available, responsive, supportive, and competent.

What message does it send our members when they know that if they call us with an emergency that we will respond appropriately and immediately? Whether pastors know it or not, members of our congregations talk to one another. Yes, the gripers are always with us and spread their "good cheer" rather often and easily. But so do those who have been faithfully served by a new pastor.

Solid and dependable pastoral care needs to be among the pastor's early goals and priorities. While it is true that such a concern should always be part of our ministry, my point here is to emphasize its importance as a critical step in establishing a ministry. When we miss an opportunity, for whatever reason, there are those who will remember; when we serve an opportunity, we make supporters and friends.

Developing Mutual Accountability

A third principle to apply to the beginning of any ministry would be to develop mutual accountability, both among and between the staff and the leadership of the church. This means that we all deliberately take responsibility for our areas of ministry, share openly what is happening in those areas, seek advice and counsel from one another, support one another, and hold one another responsible. As this mutual accountability is practiced, there begins to form a growing awareness that (*a*) ministry is what we *all* are about, not just those whom we pay to do things, and that (*b*) we as pastors value, appreciate, and welcome the counsel and support of those who are part of our fellowship.

There are various ways to accomplish this development:

- *Working toward a common vision for the ministry of the congregation.* This vision needs to come from within the organization, but it finds its articulation in the leadership of the church.
- *Developing shared goals and objectives as leaders.* We bring our gifts and talents, as well as our insights, into the community and seek to serve the needs we see there as we follow what we believe God is calling us to do and be.
- *The sharing of leadership.* Ministry is about the whole people of God serving in a shared community. We need to always be alert for potential leaders and nurture, instruct and help them to find ways to use their gifts.
- *The way we go about doing our business in the church.* Is there openness of discussion? Are people willing to listen to new ideas?

Is the dialogue healthy within the community of faith? Have we broken down the distinctions between young and old, between new members and those who have been around for a long time, as we seek to be responsive to what we feel is the challenge and call of God for this fellowship?

- *People taking responsibility for their part of the ministry and serving faithfully and committedly.* When this happens, then accountability becomes second nature to the way the church functions and ministers.

So, is there a honeymoon period at the beginning of a ministry that can be enjoyed for a while, or is the start-up of any ministry more like a trial period of testing and evaluation? The answer is probably somewhere in the middle of those extremes. Observation would seem to indicate that whatever honeymoon period there is has been shortened in our society as people seem less willing to embrace new leadership with open arms as they perhaps once were. But in both images, honeymoon or trial, getting off on the right foot is extremely important.

Which leads us to a fourth operating principle to consider, important enough to warrant a chapter unto itself: The central issue in any relationship, be it marriage, friendship, work, or ministry, is the development of trust between the persons involved. That topic will gain our full attention in the next chapter.

CHAPTER 4

Paying Your Dues
Building the Trust Fund of Trust

My first parish was in the hills of upper Appalachia in Pennsylvania. It was a two-point parish, with one of the churches in a town of about 400 people (the only church in town) and the other about five miles west nestled in a grove of trees with an old, abandoned schoolhouse across the street. The nearest drugstore was eight miles away, as was the nearest fast-food restaurant. One blinking traffic light stood at the edge of the town. A post office, general store, fire hall, and bar were the significant buildings other than the church, which was the largest of the structures.

Seminary had not prepared me for the realities of parish ministry. Sure, I was classically trained in Bible, theology, history, pastoral care, preaching, and the rest. But here I was on somewhat foreign soil and no textbook I owned was of much help. I was young, right out of seminary, energetic, raring to go, and fairly confident that I knew what being a parish pastor was all about.

My immediate predecessor was a man who died suddenly of a heart attack after serving the parish for 16 years. He was liked, respected, and poorly compensated for his efforts. How does a new pastor follow such a long-term pastorate? How does one get "into" the parish? These questions and more were rampant as I unpacked my family, books, and clothes. What needs to be done? What should I concentrate on first? Will people like me? Will they respond to my leadership? What do they expect of their new, young pastor?

A warm welcome awaited us as we drove up to the new parsonage they had just completed for us. It was a beautiful home. I was fairly convinced that they were working out their grief over the loss of their former pastor and how they had treated him (he was the third-lowest-paid pastor in our judicatory when he died) by building us a brand new 15-room home.

The pantry had been stocked and parishioners showed up at our door with chicken and watermelon that first evening.

And so, I began my first day. While unpacking books at my office, the phone rang. It was the local funeral director, who introduced himself and told me that I had a death in the parish. He gave me the particulars and I immediately called the family and made arrangements to see them. Here I was, the first day on the job, meeting a family for the first time and planning a funeral with them. I did not remember anyone from my seminary days ever telling me how to go about doing this.

On the second day in the office, I received another phone call from my new friend at the funeral home, informing me of another, unrelated death in the parish. Again, the family of the deceased was anxious to meet and talk to me. I now was faced with another family to get to know in a hurry—to pray with and plan a funeral for.

The third day arrived with the sun coming up and me hard at work on my first funeral homily. I had visited two families in two days and planned to attend the funeral visitation that day to meet the funeral director personally. By this point, I had unpacked only one box of books; the parsonage was another story altogether. As I was putting the finishing touches on the homily, guess who called? Yes, another death and another family in need of pastoral care and support. I rushed off to do what I had quickly learned to do.

During the day of my fourth day as pastor of this parish, I flinched at each phone call. The first funeral was planned, the second and third ones were in the works, and I was feeling slightly overwhelmed as I began to think about worship on that first Sunday.

I received two calls from colleagues whom I knew who had heard about the deaths through their own parishioners. One asked, "What are you doing over there?" while the other quipped, "They're just dying to see you!" Both, however, offered their support and caring to this new pastor.

Late in the evening, as I was decompressing from the load of the day, that dreaded phone call actually came. A fourth death in four days. I did what a pastor does at times like that—prayed and went to see the family.

The fifth day arrived with two funerals done and two in the works and no Sunday sermon on the horizon. A phone call did come, however—this time, fortunately, from my bishop. He obviously had heard about the extraordinary beginning of this new ministry and called to ask how I was faring amidst the unbelievable. He was very kind and supportive, but could not resist suggesting that at this rate of attrition, he would have to find me a new call in about two years. I thanked him for his concern.

There are certainly easier and better ways to begin a ministry. Obviously none of this was in my control. But three things occurred in and through all of this: First, people got to know me quickly. Word spread about this new pastor whom many of them had only met during the congregational meeting when the vote was taken to offer a call. I had gotten into people's homes and lives immediately at a time of real need for them. Second, I got to know many of the people I was called to serve very quickly as well. We prayed together. They shared stories about their loved one to help me know something about who he or she was. We laughed and cried together. And, third, that most valuable of pastoral assets, *trust*, began to develop.

Not insignificantly, one year later, when my own father died of a sudden heart attack at the age of 51, the first people who arrived at the parsonage with food, love, and condolences were these same families that I had gotten to know in their time of sorrow and loss.

To change the analogy a bit from the previous chapter, the beginning of a ministry is like paying dues to an organization. People expect something of their new pastor—good sermons, friendliness, availability, caring, to name a few. As we pay these dues, a trust fund of trust is developed. So, we need to go back a bit and ask the obvious question, "How is trust developed?"

How Trust Is Developed and Nurtured

A number of years ago, social scientist Jack Gibb articulated this exact issue in his "Trust Formation Theory." According to Gibb, whenever persons gather in a group, from two to 200 or more, there are basic concerns that may be seen as stages in trust formation. From a systematic study of hundreds of groups (therapy groups, business and social groups), Gibb worked out a theoretical model that provides a way of looking at the basic concerns and locating the problems of any group where two or three gather, including a congregation.

A Developmental Issue

Gibb's theory proposes that there are four major concerns that arise from any social interaction, whether brief or long-term: acceptance, data-flow, goal formation, and control. As these concerns are operative within each stage of trust development, there are questions that need some resolution before one can proceed to the next stage.

The questions regarding *acceptance*, for instance, manifest themselves in issues of membership: Who am I in this group? What will it cost me to belong? Will others accept me for who I am? Do I really want to belong to this group of people?

Once those questions are resolved, the person moves on to the next stage, *data-flow*, which is really the other side of the membership issue. The person poses such questions as, Who else is here? What status do the other members have here? Is there some history to this group that needs to be known?

Again, as these issues are resolved and answered, one can move to the next stage of *goal formation*, which really involves questions about productivity: What are our goals, anyway? What are we here for? What are we supposed to do together? Where are we going?

Finally, as the group moves past the third stage, the issue of *control* must be faced. These are organizational questions and issues: How are we going to accomplish our stated goal? What procedures should we use? What gifts and talents are there here to take us to where we should be going? Who are our leaders?

Although any or all of these questions may be operative in a group of people at any given moment, they tend to manifest themselves as primary concerns in a chronological hierarchy. In other words, satisfaction or resolution in each stage in sequence is necessary before the group can profitably move on to the next stage.

This theory can also be used diagnostically within a group. For instance, in watching a group of people, if the members of the group are experiencing difficulty in determining how to proceed in implementing their goal (issues of control), the source of that difficulty can be found in the unfinished business of the stage before it, that is, goal formation. If members are unable to agree about their agenda or purpose, then their data-flow has been inadequate, so that the unresolved issues regarding who they are with one another have blocked commitment to a common goal. If there is restricted or obstructed data-flow, the reason can be found in the area of acceptance, where at least one (if not more) member of the group does not feel sufficiently accepted to be able even to hear the sharing from other members. Until basic communications can be established, further work is actually impossible for the group as a whole.

Can this theory be applied to churches? Certainly—and even to functioning groups within a congregation. The theory offers us a handle for understanding how groups and persons within groups function. A congregation is a collection of people subject to the same stages of development as any group of persons. A new pastor coming into a congregation would be well served to understand something about this developmental theory so as to appreciate the issues he or she is facing.

Trust, simply put, takes time. A group must work its way through these stages so as to be able to articulate and achieve its stated goals and mission. A congregation where people are leaving and joining will always be working on the formation of trust as the faces in the group change over time.

Why Does It Take So Long?

I repeat: Trust, in any relationship, simply takes time. Let us start there. Think of the relationships you have entered into, with spouse or friends. It takes time to answer those initial-stage questions. The only way we really get to know someone is if they self-disclose, that is, share something of who they are and what they think and feel. In beginning relationships, this is always risky business. None of us is ever sure if what we share will be honored, respected, and accepted by another until we take the plunge. Trust develops as more is shared and the sharing becomes mutual.

In other words, for you to get to know me there needs to be significant encounters of sharing so that trust can form between us. This rarely happens immediately or fast.

Extrapolate that example to a pastor coming into a congregation for a moment. How does a congregation get to know a pastor? Obviously, this happens as the pastor shares him- or herself—in visits, newsletters, letters, sermons, greetings between services, and so on.

But how frequent are those opportunities for sharing in a congregation? Probably the majority of parishioners only have contact with their pastors on a regular basis on Sunday mornings. Those previously mentioned crises can increase those pastoral contacts and, as noted previously, are excellent opportunities for mutual sharing. Regular home visitation of members of the parish also increases those contact times. In certain settings, however, those regular home visits are harder and harder to accomplish. In suburbia, for instance, where I currently serve, the majority of households consist of two working parents with children in more activities than the family can adequately manage and still keep their sanity. Home calls, when done, are usually for purposes of church business or specific pastoral need. Rarely do they occur for social purposes of simply getting to know the people, and often happen in the evenings between soccer practice and grocery shopping. The day and age of a pastor simply "dropping in" on a parishioner's home is long gone in this pastoral setting.

So, if trust is built as interpersonal sharing takes place, and, within a congregation, those opportunities are infrequent, it is a foregone conclusion that such trust formation will take considerable time. As stated in a previous chapter, folk wisdom has said that it takes five to seven years for such trust to develop and for the pastor to feel like he or she has "arrived." Maybe now we can understand some of the reasons why.

Moving beyond the theory of trust formation, let us look specifically at four issues under the rubric of "paying your dues." These four issues, if dealt with well, can go a long way in establishing trust between a pastor and a congregation.

Issue #1: Picking the Battles to Fight

When talking about battles to fight, two metaphors come immediately to mind for a pastor just beginning in a call: There are only so many bullets in the gun and only so many dollars in the wallet. Newly arrived pastors would do well to keep in mind either of those images. Truthfully, pastors have limited bullets and/or currency to use in fighting battles within the parish. Using them wisely is sage advice.

Also, truth be told, not every struggle, battle, or disagreement is worth being crucified over. Choosing which battles we are willing to fight and which ones we are willing to concede is good common sense and smart ministry. It shows others that we can listen to another's ideas and opinions and be reasonable in our response to them.

Let me offer one example from my experience in this current call. (Actually, I used the story before, but with a different point to make; bear with me a moment.) As I stated earlier, I was called here to give leadership to a major building project, which involved a new worship space, offices, choir room, narthex, and expanded parking lot. The building committee was solid, chaired by a long-time member with engineering experience.

Anyone who has ever been involved in a building program knows there are many decisions to be made. The building committee always made good decisions, it seemed to me, but never easily. They debated every issue into the ground.

I was very careful about my ideas and opinions. First of all, this was our building, not Glenn Ludwig's building. Second, the church had other changes that needed to be made, specifically in the area of worship, that I suspected would be battles. Therefore, I was not going to use all my currency on the building project only to discover an empty wallet when it came time to tackle some important issues, like the frequency of communion and liturgical practices.

Issue # 2: Losing with Grace

Continuing the storyline as an illustration to this concept, the building plan was to do the construction in two phases, a year or so apart (I have already outlined the story in chapter 2). Suffice it to say for this present point that I didn't think that was a wise decision. So, I talked the building committee into polling the congregation about doing the whole thing at once. It would save money, time, and fuss. The congregation resoundingly defeated my idea.

Now, it was important for me as a new pastor to lose this battle with grace. First, as I said before, it was *our* building, not mine. It was something we all needed to own, both the building and the process for completing it. Second, I trusted the leaders of this project. They believed we needed to do it over time. I challenged that assumption and lost, but we all gained, for in going to the congregation it reaffirmed the earlier decision of two phases. And third, I trusted that God would guide and lead us. If the time was not right, then pushing and shoving would have served no purpose whatsoever.

Losing a battle with grace shows maturity in the long run. It says, "I may not agree, but the wisdom and wishes of the congregation are part of why I serve here. Let's move on."

One caveat is needed to this discussion of battles and losing with grace. If we strongly disagree about a decision but lose the battle, it is altogether appropriate to revisit that issue at a later time, but such revisiting must be done rationally, creatively, and prayerfully. A demeanor and attitude that shows maturity will go a long way in getting another hearing of the issue in question.

You may rightly ask if I did that in regard to the two-phase decision. I will answer, "No." I came to believe over time that it was indeed the right decision for this congregation to make at the time. My prayerful deliberations after losing the battle also led me to believe that God had a better plan than mine in mind. God indeed did.

Issue # 3: Winning as a Team Victory

Ultimately, being in parish ministry is not about winning and losing. It is about service—to God, to one another, to the community, and to the world.

Whenever decisions are made within any organization, those decisions need to be supported and affirmed by those affected by the decisions. In a congregational setting, when decisions are made in a leadership body (committee, council, board), we all win when we can affirm and support them.

In our congregations, we have an added strength to take into account as we discuss and make decisions. God's will and purpose for us as Christ's church is very much a part of all we do. Personally, I do not believe we are puppets for God to manipulate. We are free to make our decisions as we feel we must. But as a community of God's people, we seek God's guidance and wisdom in all we do. And we believe God can even use our dumbest decisions to serve God's will. Faithfully serving God means we all win in the long run.

Issue # 4: Effecting Change

The final issue in regards to "paying your dues" has more to do with a "down payment" on the future than with meeting some sort of obligation. Effecting change in an organization, like an established congregation, is an important role for any person called into a leadership position. Change is inevitable. Effecting healthy change is, therefore, one of the challenges of effective leadership and ministry.

Ronald A. Heifetz, director of the Leadership Education Project at the John F. Kennedy School of Government at Harvard University, in his engaging book *Leadership without Easy Answers*, begins his lengthy treatise with these prophetic words: "Today we face a crisis in leadership in many areas of public and private life."[1] Gil Rendle, vice president for program at the Alban Institute, echoes this sentiment and applies it to our congregations: "Questions are also being raised about the quality and competence of those, both clergy and lay, who are serving as leaders in our congregations."[2]

There is strong consensus about that leadership is a necessary quality of ministry. People look to us to be leaders. Writing in *The Christian Century*, L. Gregory Jones and Susan Pendleton Jones, of Duke Divinity School, state, "Effective congregations share one other feature: wise pastoral leadership."[3]

However, there is no clear consensus regarding what leadership is. Heifetz maintains that leadership is "mobilizing people to tackle tough problems."[4] The United States Army defines leadership as "influencing people—by providing purpose, direction, and motivation—while operating to accomplish the mission and improving the organization." Rendle makes a helpful distinction between management and leadership: "Management asks the question, 'Are we doing things right?' . . . leadership asks the question, 'Are we doing the right things?'"[5] James Burns, political scientist and historian, in his 1978 study *Leadership*, distinguished between two styles of leadership—transactional and transformational. The relations of most leaders and followers are *transactional*—leaders approach followers with an eye toward exchanging one thing for another. It is the old *quid pro quo* of human interactions. On the other hand, *transforming* leadership is more potent because the leader seeks to satisfy higher needs in the followers and engages them in a much more energetic and fulfilling way. In a sense, transformational leadership is the elevation of aspiration and leads to the conversion of followers into leaders and leaders into moral agents. Finally, management expert Ken Blanchard has offered an effective model, called Situational Leadership, which identifies four leadership styles: directive, coaching, supporting, and delegating.

The important point for our purposes in this chapter is that leadership is an essential quality for effecting change in a congregation. Anthony Robinson, pastor of Plymouth Congregational Church (UCC) in Seattle, reflects on Burns's *Leadership* study and applies it to congregational life:

> Ministry that operates only at the transactional level—meeting expressed needs—may fail to touch the deepest needs of congregations and of the people who make them up: the need for transformation, for personal and institutional change in light of the

vision and values of the gospel. Clergy who operate only at the transactional level are in danger of allowing the congregation to become an audience or clientele for goods and services. The priesthood of all believers becomes the gathering of religious consumers.[6]

So, ministry is about transformation and transformation is about change. How does a pastor effect change from his or her position of leadership? That question has been the subject of many articles and books. There is not enough time and space to deal adequately with that topic in this chapter. It is sufficient for us to note that effecting change in healthy and creative ways is a down payment on the future relationship between a pastor and a congregation. Pastors can effect such changes through many styles and forms, and through a multitude of understandings about leadership. The plethora of quotes about leadership used in this chapter was to whet your appetite for further investigation. The fact remains, however, that effecting such changes in our congregations is one of our important leadership roles.

CHAPTER 5

Building the Pillars as Foundations

Research on Long-Term Pastorates

For many years now, the Alban Institute has offered a seminar titled "New Visions for the Long Pastorate." From research and consultations, Alban has identified five pillars that are needed to support effective long-term pastorates.[1] This chapter will examine each of those five pillars and offer comment based on my own experience. The seminar was very helpful to me 10 years ago when I took it and I have had many opportunities to reflect on those five pillars that were identified. Here, then, are those five pillars and comment from a decade of striving to build and maintain them.

Pillar #1: Monitoring Burnout

The most important quality we have as people in ministry is our vitality. Energy and health are very important aspects of pastoral effectiveness. Therefore, we need to be good stewards of ourselves. The ministry will take every ounce of effort and time we choose to give it.

It has been widely understood that only 20 percent of communication takes place through words. Therefore, 80 percent of what we seek to communicate is nonverbal. If proclamation through preaching, teaching, and pastoral care help define our roles, then the person who has vitality and joy will be a more effective instrument of that proclamation.

The inaugural issue of *Church Executive* magazine has as its lead article "Clergy Burnout." In this article, managing editor Shannon L. Pearson quotes an amazing statistic: "According to the Samaritan Institute,[2] approximately 1,300 pastors leave the profession monthly."[3] Certainly retirements are a part of that figure. The vast majority, however, simply leave the ministry to pursue other careers. Pearson writes: "The Pastors Institute in Indianapolis recently concluded a study in which it asked those who recently left the pastorate their reasons for leaving, and the results were astounding. The top three reasons cited by former ministers included disillusionment, fatigue, and burnout, and the need to resign in order to leave a stressful situation."[4]

Defining Burnout

Stress and burnout have become rather chic terms in our culture. Everyone talks about how busy they are, how stressed out their lives are, or how nearing burnout they have become. But we should first define what these terms mean. Just because someone works hard does not mean that they will automatically suffer burnout.

Let us start with *stress*. Stress is a factor in clergy lives early on in a ministry (some say the first 10 years or so), a by-product of dealing with all the newness, the novelty, and the change as one begins a call. It is the strain that we feel on our physical, psychological, emotional, and, yes, spiritual selves. It is the pressure we know only too well as we seek to be faithful to our calls.

Burnout occurs after the novelty and newness wear off and it can be lethal to effective ministry. Burnout makes us dull, hollow, empty, and uninteresting people. Alban estimates that one out of five clergy suffer from burnout.

Perhaps the best definition of burnout comes from preacher and teacher William Willimon in a book he wrote years ago as part of Lyle Schaller's "Creative Leadership Series." In it, Willimon refers to an earlier work by John A. Sanford, *Ministry Burnout*. Here is Willimon referencing Sanford, "John Sanford suggests that the phenomenon of dissipation and disengagement, which we commonly call burnout, may arise from a lack of meaning rather than from a lack of energy. I agree. . . . In other words, people appear to burn out in the church not necessarily because they are overworked, but because they are overburdened with the trivial and the unimportant."[5]

Willimon's words offer an insightful and helpful understanding of the term. In the world of work, burnout occurs when energy is expended without fuel being added. The fuel that supplies the energy to minister is a conviction that what we do has meaning and importance. Our energy—so important to ministry, as we have already noted—to stay committed to our callings stays high because what we do and who we are makes some sense to us. When we no longer find meaning, even the smallest of pastoral actions can drain us. Burnout, rightly understood, is the result of the lack of meaning in what we do.

The Effect of Stress on Burnout

If burnout occurs after the novelty of a situation has worn off, it is obvious that stress plays an initial part in its possible occurrence. Stress, in a sense, can be a precursor to burnout.

There are a few notable distinctions between the two that can diagnostically assist a pastor in monitoring where they are. Stress, for instance, comes as a result of overuse of our adjustment capacities. Burnout, on the other hand, comes from the overuse of our listening and caring capacities. Whereas stress is a result of too much change, flux, newness, and novelty, burnout is a result of too much responsibility and too many needy people who demand or expect our attention and time.

It is commonly acknowledged that stress can result in one or more of the following: loss of perception, loss of options, regression to non-adult behaviors, and/or physical illness. Burnout can result in one or more of these conditions: physical and/or emotional exhaustion, cynicism, disillusionment, and/or self-deprecation.

Burnout is really a disease of the over-committed and, among professionals, pastors by their very sense of call are among the most committed to their vocations. It goes without saying that all of us must do our ministries within the confines of the human body and all bodies have limitations. Individually, those limitations caused by stress and over-commitment can slow us down and make us ineffective. And if we draw out that metaphor and use it collectively, a pastor with burnout will affect the communal body of the church in negative ways. Burnout affects, in other words, not just the pastor, but the pastor's family and the congregation.

The Burnout Cycle

The Alban Institute has described a "Burnout Cycle" which offers us yet more handles on this phenomenon (fig. 1).[6] Since it is self-explanatory, I present it here without further comment.

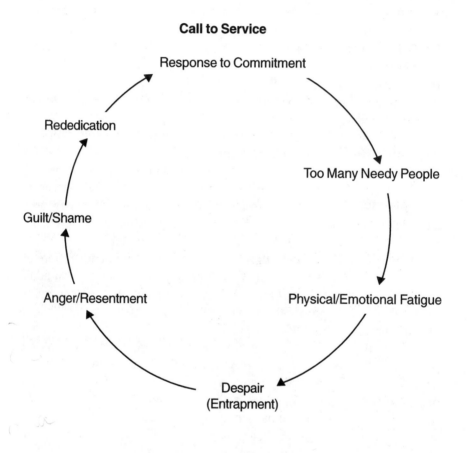

Figure 1: Burnout Cycle

Strategies to Deal with Burnout

If vitality for life and ministry is linked to effectiveness, then anything we do to increase our physical, psychological, mental, and spiritual health will help us in monitoring burnout. The following list of self-care strategies is meant to be suggestive and not exhaustive. The more of these strategies we employ in our ministries, the better chance we have of staying fresh and energized to fulfill our callings. (There are many helpful and valuable books available on this topic; check the resource list at the end of this book for suggestions.)

a. *Spiritual Formation.* This has to do with remembering who we are and whose we are. If burnout is a loss of meaning, then remembering what it is we are called to be and do will always serve us well. Scripture reading, meditation, prayer, reflection, and retreats can all help to remind us of what we are to be doing and of God's promises to us.

b. *Time Out.* Role ambiguity can lead us to over-extending ourselves. Times of rest are very important. The concept of sabbath time is a commandment to rest from daily labors. It is important to find those times of refreshment by taking regular days off and using our vacations. Extended times away should also be planned. The development of a sabbatical policy in the congregation is a good idea. It is wise to develop such a policy with the governing board early in one's ministry so that they can help educate and prepare the congregation in advance of taking the sabbatical. Roy Oswald's video, *Why You Should Give Your Pastor a Sabbatical,*[7] helped the congregation I serve to develop its policy for all staff. The key here to any time away—whether it is a vacation, or a day or two a week, or an extended sabbatical—is to use the time to restore vitality.

c. *Support Network.* Finding other pastors who are willing to share in the struggles and joys of ministry is very supportive. It is important that these pastors be people that can be trusted so that sharing can be open and honest. I believe that this is such an important strategy for the health of pastors that I have dedicated the next chapter to this topic.

d. *Regular Exercise.* There is no better antidote to depression than exercise. We need to get those endorphins working for us in positive ways.

e. *Therapy.* There are times in ministry when the help and support of a trained professional may be needed to restore balance and vitality.

This is especially true if cynicism gets too deep or too prolonged. A good therapist can help us to deal with those issues that we cannot deal with in the context of our parishes. I have been fortunate to have had the help of competent counselors over the years; I dare say that they have helped to keep me balanced and functional during some difficult times.

f.   *A New Interest.* Sometimes we need a boost of sorts in our ministry. There are times when a new project can offer us that. An avocation can bring renewed vitality into our lives. And sometimes this happens outside of our ministry and ends up energizing us for that ministry.

All of these strategies are meant to raise our level of health, which is the best way to fight off burnout.

Pillar # 2: Balancing Individual and Corporate Needs (The Gap Theory)

Once one has built trust in the congregation, what effect does that trust have on congregational leadership? The Gap Theory[8] seeks to explain the relationship between trust that develops through individual encounters in a congregation and trust that develops as a pastor assumes leadership within the congregation (corporate trust).

In graph form, the Gap Theory looks something like figure 2:

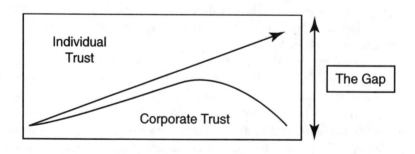

Figure 2: The Gap Theory

Individual trust really is about a pastor's credibility. As we have said previously, such trust develops over time and is greatly increased when a pastor deals compassionately and competently with crises. The longer a pastor serves in one place, the more opportunities there are to minister in crises, and the more members will come to trust, respect, and like the pastor.

Corporate trust has to do with the confidence the congregation, especially the leaders of that congregation, has in the pastor as a leader. Can we be trusted in decision making? Can we be the leaders they need? Can we push, pull, guide, and challenge in healthy and appropriate ways? And can we deal with the conflict that naturally arises from change?

Developing Credibility

The gap occurs when a pastor pays more attention to individual needs than to corporate needs. It is an easy gap to fall into. As our individual relationships with parishioners grow and trust develops, we may tend to avoid the difficult corporate decisions because it might involve change and conflict with those very people with whom we have developed caring and trusting relationships.

Let me give you a simplistic example from my own ministry. The congregation council and the staff decided years ago to stop offering a New Year's Eve worship service. It had been in place for about 10 years, peaked in attendance and support after about three years, and was on a slow but steady decline. After the Advent and Christmas services, the staff was exhausted. We all needed some time off and away. There was little enthusiasm for doing this extra service when less than 1 percent of the congregation attended.

So, we made the decision to cancel the service, which we properly announced to the congregation in a newsletter article. Consequently, I received a phone call from a parishioner who had become a friend and for whom I had ministered through two health crises. He complained loudly. This was an important service for him. He was grateful for what God and the church had done for him in his moment of need during the past year and was looking forward to that service to give thanks and to pray for a healthy new year. My pastoral conscience was tweaked by his appeal. I understood because I knew his recent pain. And I caved in.

Because of one sincere, persistent, and needy voice, I offered to do the service. I found an organist who was also willing and we offered the worship experience. The parishioner and his whole family attended, but very few others. I had let my individual trust get in the way of a corporate decision. (One can easily argue that a pastor should always meet the individual needs and, therefore, this example breaks down at that point. However, my point was to illustrate how the gap theory worked in at least one instance.)

I will tell you that this same man was adamantly opposed to building a new worship space, which we desperately needed to do. I listened to his pleas, shared his letters of protest with the council, and took his concerns seriously. But we built anyway. Three years into the use of the new space, he confessed to me that he had been wrong and congratulated me on my faithfulness and persistence in leadership.

Sometimes pastors and leaders in a congregation allow their personal relationships to get in the way of difficult changes and decisions. I've known churches where it only took one dissenting voice to scuttle an idea. When that happens, we give veto power to every single person in the congregation and the gap theory is put into practice at its extreme.

Factors That Feed into the Gap

A number of factors can feed into the gap and help it to widen and deepen. The first is just plain *exhaustion*. As has already been stated, we work hard to get ourselves established in ministry. There is so much to be done and so much to learn. We listen intently to how things have always been done, spend time educating for needed changes, and then begin to push those changes in place. All of this takes a toll on us. A pastor beginning a ministry will often find him- or herself exhausted after five or seven years of doing this.

Another factor that feeds into the gap has to do with *quality feedback*. The longer a pastor is in place, the more relationships of trust and respect that have been established, the harder it is to get accurate information from people. No one wants to hurt the pastor's feelings, especially if they like the pastor. So, the members of the parish may stop expecting so much from us.

This factor can become lethal in the long term. In fact, one of the pillars to building an effective long-term pastorate is this whole issue of quality feedback (a topic that comes up later in this chapter).

A third factor, which is really related to the first one, is that *the pastor simply gets tired of pushing.* Exhaustion can lead to this, as can the friendships that have developed. No matter what causes it, the pastor gets tired of always being the front person for change. It is easier to go along and not make the changes that can lead to conflict and unease.

However, the ministry is not a place of rest. It is a calling to faithfulness. The pastor needs to be the prophetic voice, the one who calls the people of God into accountability. That is never an easy role, but one that is a very important part of our callings.

Another factor goes back to the trust theory of group development mentioned in a previous chapter. If trust needs to be formed before any group can become functional and effective, then *every pastor needs to develop individual trust before corporate trust can be established.* In other words, the people of our congregations have to like and respect us as individuals before they will trust us with corporate and communal decisions.

We develop that individual trust over time in a variety of ways. But as that trust, needed for corporate trust, is developed, we can easily fall into the gap and become ineffective in the corporate life of the church. It is an easy gap to fall into, as we have noted.

The Danger of "Going Native"

One further factor that can contribute to the gap must be mentioned—the pastor "going native." Certainly a pastor needs to understand and appreciate the cultural values and mores of the people among whom he or she is called to serve. But when a pastor appropriates those values—that is, goes native— the pastor loses the credibility to be prophetic as God's word challenges the lives of God's people. To appropriate the native culture is to lose that prophetic voice.

The other danger of going native has to do with our ability to lead. If a pastor goes native, his or her expectations of the people will be no larger than their own expectations. Like it or not, the pastoral role is one of vision and the development of a consensus of that vision. We need to challenge our people constantly to go deeper, farther, and longer than they are sometimes comfortable going. The pastor, in a sense, leads the charge and it is difficult to do that when the credibility of our office has given way to being liked, accepted, and admired. And the longer a pastor is in one setting, the easier this temptation becomes.

The pastor in a long-term call must constantly work to balance individual trust and corporate responsibility. Otherwise, the gap becomes a reality and we lose our effectiveness as called leaders.

Pillar #3: Balancing Power and Decision Making

It probably goes without saying that the longer a pastor serves in a parish, the more powerful that pastor becomes. This is not a value statement but a truthful observation. Power is not necessarily a bad thing. It takes power and influence to get many things done in a parish. It is part of all human relationships and group dynamics.

The reasons that power accumulates naturally over time are numerous. They include, but are not limited to the following:

- the forming of relationships that result in trust;
- the amount of "currency" the pastor accumulates and does not spend over time;
- the fact that knowledge is power and that the longer a pastor is in place, the more knowledge about the organization, the history, and the value system the pastor gains; and
- over time, the pastor really becomes the bearer of tradition, as the lay leadership changes every few years.

Therefore, the pastor really needs to work hard to balance these issues of power, control, and decision making. It is not the pastor's church, after all. It is God's church with God's people as the body.

The Two Congregations in Every Congregation

One could argue that some churches consist of more than one or two congregations. If a church has multiple worship services, there is the strong likelihood of also having multiple congregations where people from the early service do not know people who attend a later service. This is true where I serve; I am constantly introducing people to one another, both of whom have been members for a number of years.

However, as we consider issues of power, control, leadership, and decision making, there really are only two congregations in every church. There is a larger congregation whom we shall call Congregation B, and a smaller group within that congregation, called Congregation A. Figure 3 offers a simple diagram to illustrate something of the dynamics of these two groups:[9]

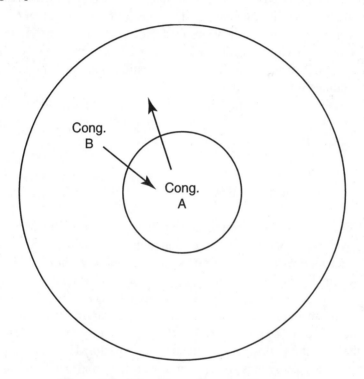

Figure 3: The Two Congregations

The larger group, Congregation B, normally is content simply to worship. They are not much interested in the politics of the church, serving in any leadership position, or the decisions of the board or council. These are the followers who, by and large, are content to go along with what the leaders want. Just do not mess with their worship time or change their worship experience or expectations too much and you have a group of contented followers.

As a pastor, the majority of our leadership work, and, therefore, the majority of our time, except for crises and pastoral care issues that affect both groups, is spent working with Congregation A. This is the core of any church. If we need something done, these are the folks we naturally ask to do it. Congregation A is the backbone of the church, giving in support of the budget up to 80 percent of the monies given.

The arrows on the diagram suggest that there is flow from one Congregation into the other. Naturally that is the case. A person volunteers or is invited to serve in leadership and thereby joins Congregation A. When their service time is over or they simply decide not to serve any longer, they move back into Congregation B. Later, perhaps, they may return to Congregation A or they will leave Congregation B at your church to join Congregation B down the road somewhere.

It is obviously a very fluid relationship, or at least it should be. The line encircling Congregation A should be porous, enabling members of Congregation B to have access and entrance.

When the Core Begins to Shrink

There is a natural phenomenon that happens when a pastor serves in a parish over a span of time. The core, Congregation A, will become smaller. This is an automatic and natural occurrence in any church. The core becomes smaller and more homogeneous. And this has nothing to do with trying to manipulate the system. That manipulation can happen, of course, but the movement toward a common mindset is natural and to be expected.

The core can also begin to reflect the age, value system, theology, and even the working philosophy of the long-term pastor. This occurs, partly, because as the pastor gains power over time, those persons in Congregation B, who may have a different voice or view, will not come forward to join Congregation A. They either will not feel comfortable, will not fit in, or they just do not have the strength, courage, or time to challenge the in-bredness of Congregation A.

Keeping Democracy Alive

The danger, therefore, is that Congregation A becomes ingrown. Only those who reflect the pastor's ideas, values, and theology are either welcome or are comfortable being a part of the inner core. People in Congregation B begin to see that their perspective, their viewpoints, and their ideas are not represented in the decision making of the core. This can lead not only to less people from Congregation B moving into Congregation A, it can also cause some resentment of the leadership and the pastor. At the extreme, for those who could and should move into leadership, it can be frustrating and can lead to them moving on to another church or even forsaking church involvement altogether.

The answer to the problems caused by this natural occurrence is for the pastor and the leadership to keep democracy alive. Vigilance is needed to make sure that variety is represented on boards and committees. It is a general rule of thumb that when people feel impotent they will use their power and influence in negative ways.

The longer a pastor serves in a call not only does power build and the possibility of a shrinking core occur, but the pastor also knows more and more people. That knowledge can assist the pastor in helping keep democracy alive.

The Leadership Role of the Pastor over Time

One of the ways a pastor can use his or her accumulated power and influence is in seeing that there is balance on boards and committees. Is there an equal representation of longer-term members of the congregation and new members to the community? Are women represented fairly on governing boards, and not just on the education committee? Is there a good age spread among those who serve?

The pastor can influence not only who gets asked to serve, but the pastor can also be the main influence in asking people to serve. I have always taken seriously my role as chief recruiter and cheerleader for the ministry. First, if we are not excited and articulate about the ministry, how can we expect the same from lay people? Second, as a pastor here for a long time, I know more people than anyone in the church. I am in the best position to evaluate a person's gifts and heart. And I have learned over time never to say no for anyone.

This vigilance for prospective leadership can take many practical forms. I keep notecards tucked into the back of my hymnal and, as I pray about our ministries in worship and look out over the faces, I jot down potential people for those leadership roles. I pray through our membership list on a regular basis and, in that process, discover names of people to contact, both for pastoral care and concern, and for possible leadership roles. I am constantly seeking the best people to serve on decision-making bodies: people with commitment, dedication, and gifts. Sometimes these folks may not even have considered being in leadership, that is, moving from Congregation A to Congregation B. My invitation may be just the impetus they need to grow in their discipleship and in the use of their God-given gifts.

The Dynamics of Shared Leadership

Once a gifted and committed person has been asked and has agreed to serve in leadership, the other leaders, and especially the pastor, have the responsibility of bringing that person "on board." Orientation sessions can give the new member a sense of the history of the organization or committee they have agreed to serve. If mission and vision statements exist, it is important to share them. Core values of the group, which help it to do its work, are also good to share. All of these items can give a new leader a sense of where the group has been and perhaps a hint about where it wants to go. Knowledge, as they say, is power and the balancing of power is the goal to establishing this important pillar for a long-term pastorate.

It is also good to share with the new leader a sense of the expectations of time and energy. For instance, as we began our major building project, I made sure that new council members understood that there would probably be the need for extra meetings. We also recruited persons who were wholeheartedly in favor of the project. Once a decision is made to go ahead, it is frustrating and time wasting to have to rehash that decision at every meeting because the people who have been asked to serve do not agree with the direction that had already been set. Although it sounds like control, it is simply good management of time and resources. Assuming that everyone had many opportunities to debate, discuss, and argue over a project, once the decision is made, it is time to move forward and not stop work every time someone raises a dissenting voice again.

We have talked about leadership and the role of the pastor before, but another word is in order at this point. The pastor as leader sets the tone and the pace for the rest of the leaders of the congregation. Is there an openness to discuss and consider new ideas? Is there accountability for ministry at all levels of the congregation, the laity as well as the clergy? Is there ongoing support and encouragement for those who serve and seek to use their gifts? Is there a sense of vision that will move the congregation forward as it seeks to serve God and the community? The pastor will set the tone for that to happen through his or her writings, sermons, teachings, and discussions.

As the committed leaders are called, educated, and supported, balancing power and decision making will go a long way in keeping a ministry fresh and vibrant. This all happens when leadership is shared appropriately and dynamically.

Pillar # 4: Seeking Quality Feedback

A fourth pillar needing attention and energy if a long-term pastorate is going to continue to be effective is the need for quality feedback of the ministry. This is tough, tough work. The personal relationships, the interpersonal currency accumulated, and the building of trust all mitigate against receiving the quality feedback we need to grow, change, and continue to be effective. One needs to be diligent and vigilant in securing feedback.

Unfortunately, many congregations use only performance evaluations as a way to go about this. Performance evaluations can be a way to evaluate the functions of a staff member, especially if that person has program responsibilities. It is fairly easy, for instance, to assess whether a Vacation Bible School program has been effective by looking at attendance over the years, getting feedback from those who attended, and by asking for feedback from those who used to participate but who dropped out.

The problem with performance appraisals, however, is the faulty assumption that underlies the reasons for doing an evaluation in the first place. Most performance evaluations are done under the misguided assumption that when someone hears what she or he is *not* doing, then he or she will automatically change and do it. The assumption here was overstated, of course, but we can see where such an assumption would lead. This evaluation, in a sense, sets up the person and can be used to scapegoat a situation.

So, let us look at some basic healthy assumptions regarding clergy evaluations (we will discuss the issue of staff supervision and evaluations in a later chapter).

Basic Assumptions about Clergy Evaluations

First, we need to understand that *clergy evaluations are not a rational process*. Therefore, secular technologies in this field will not work well in a parish evaluation process. The whole issue of evaluations is charged with baggage because of the nature of parish ministry. A clergyperson may be a horrible preacher and a sloppy administrator, but a faithful and caring pastor to the people, who visits the sick and shut-ins, who responds immediately to crisis, and who genuinely cares for the individual needs of the people. Such a pastor builds a mountain of individual trust, but the leadership may see only glaring weaknesses in administration and leadership. In an evaluation process, those who have been faithfully served by this caring pastor will give that pastor a glowing evaluation, while those who need and look for leadership will be very disappointed. In a word, this is not a rational process. It is highly personal and heavily laden with baggage.

Second, it is *the pastor who needs to take the initiative in calling for an evaluation process*. Here is that whole issue of pastoral leadership again. The purpose of the feedback is so that the ministry can continue to be effective, vital, and alive. By calling for an evaluation process, the pastor demonstrates that he or she is looking for quality feedback which will help that to happen.

Third, *ministry evaluations are to be preferred over clergy evaluations*. If the ministry in a congregation is truly shared, there is a need to be mutually accountable for that ministry. It is the responsibility of the leadership of any church, which includes the laity, to see that the mission of the church is carried out. Therefore, conducting a ministry evaluation rather than a clergy one is a far better path to take. A ministry evaluation allows for shared accountability and responsibility. If there are issues that need to be addressed, there is a sense in which everyone is in the fight together. The likelihood of scapegoating is also diminished through a ministry evaluation where all take responsibility.

Fourth, it has been noted by church consultants that *those who need feedback the most are often the least able to handle that feedback psychologically*. The result is a wounded pastor who will withdraw even further, flee, or fight. The question becomes, How can a congregation, and especially its leadership, be sensitive to the pastor and at the same time offer feedback that will help the ministry grow?

Fifth, there is a *difference between role and function in ministry and that is important to understand*. It is fairly easy to evaluate the functions of a pastor. We look at the job descriptions, examine any goals that the pastor may have identified for the year, look at the statistics of each of the functions of ministry (if there are any available), and make our judgments. For instance, if a function of the pastor is to visit all the member households of the parish, it is easy to assess whether that, indeed, happened over the course of the year.

However, the ministry is really more about a role than about functions. Certainly, ministry goals and objectives can be identified and evaluated as to completion and effectiveness, but there is more to ministry than simply recording statistics of visits made. There is the role of pastor—shepherd, leader, counselor, guide, visionary, coach, cheerleader, prophet, priest, and human being. How does a congregation evaluate the role of the pastor in addition to looking at the functions that he or she has performed?

Two Kinds of Evaluations

Two kinds of evaluations can be helpful in a congregational setting. One is for administrative purposes and the other is for the purpose of individual growth and development. Let us take these one at a time and briefly comment on them.

The evaluation done for *administrative purposes* is taken on for the sake of the organization. The end result will be that the congregation is better served. Often these types of evaluations are used for budgetary development, especially salary decisions, although they do not necessarily have to be tied to those decisions. The evaluation of this kind asks the question, Is the ministry of the congregation being served?

The evaluation for *individual growth and development* should be done at a time other than budget time. The purpose is to secure quality feedback that will assist the pastor or staff member in assessing his or her personal ministries. Strengths and growth areas are identified with the purpose of helping the pastor to develop further skills and enhance the ones that need work. For instance, when I first came to my current call, I had come from a university setting. One of the functions I was asked to do in my new call was weekly children's sermons. With my own children grown and after five years of dealing with college-age students, those sermons were, indeed, weakly done. An evaluation at the end of my first year pointed this out very clearly to me. I needed to grow in that ministry. So, I read other people's sermons to children and, frankly, was not impressed. Further (and this is the key, I found), I took it upon myself to get to know the children of the parish. Obviously, this is something every pastor should do, but, depending on the size of the congregation, that task may need to be intentional, as it was with me. I targeted families with young children to visit and deliberately engaged those children in conversation over those visits. This may not have resulted in the most sterling children's sermons, but I did a much better job of relating the stories of scripture to the young lives I had gotten to know and love. The yearly evaluation led to growth for me.

Doing Role Evaluations with Your Leadership

Sometimes with our leadership group, we clergy tend to focus on getting the tasks of the church organized, completed, and evaluated. Obviously, this is what the leadership is called to do.

However, it is often helpful, informative, and enriching to do role evaluations with the congregational leadership, that is, the board, council, consistory. What would happen if once a year we would take the time to evaluate each other—council and pastor? Three questions could be thrown out for discussion: (1) What would you like more of from me? (2) What would you like less of from me? and (3) What should we keep the same?

The direction of the questions could then be reversed and pastors would reflect thoughtfully on what more we would like from our leaders, what we would like less, and what should remain the same. Such a discussion would go a long way in developing a climate of openness, trust, and growth.

Every four or five years, a broader segment of the congregation should be engaged in an evaluation of ministry. In a moment, we shall look at one way to do this. For our purposes here, suffice it to say that the goal of such an evaluation, regardless of the process used, would be to receive feedback on three important and overarching areas of parish ministry: preaching and teaching, fellowship, and service/outreach. It is also a good idea to consider using an outside consultant to design and lead this type of evaluation process.

Making the "Pinch" Theory Work

One of the ways to do an ongoing evaluation of ministry between the four or five years of a more extensive feedback process would be to use what has been labeled the "Pinch" Theory every six months or so with the leadership board. Also called Planned Renegotiation, in graph form the theory looks something like figure 4:

The "Pinch" Theory

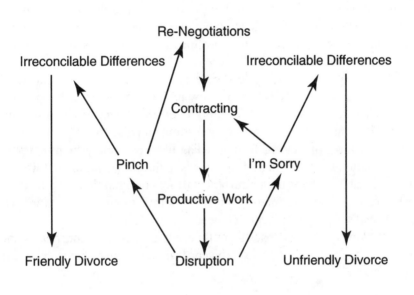

Figure 4: Planned Re-Negotiation

There is not enough space for the purposes of this book to explicate the theory here. Suffice it to say that the leadership board and the pastor could take some time about every six months and ask the question: "Where is this relationship pinching for you?" Because laypeople do not like to evaluate their pastor, this pinch theory can be an effective way to discuss mutually where changes need to be made and to agree on how to go about implementing those changes.

The Use of Focus Groups

A concept that is growing in use in congregations is focus groups. To evaluate a particular ministry or to explore a new direction in ministry, a list of carefully crafted questions is put together. Then, groups of people are invited to come together to discuss and give feedback to the questions and issues. These focus groups (named because they focus on a specific ministry or opportunity) can be heterogeneously or homogeneously chosen. Furthermore, it is a good idea to have two people present from the group desiring feedback, one to ask the questions and keep the discussion focused and the other to take notes.

The use of focus groups can be very valuable in securing intentional feedback. It is certainly better than any mailed, written evaluation sent to homes where the return rate is rarely over 20 percent of those sent and there is no chance for dialogue, explanation, and discussion.

This form of getting feedback has been extremely helpful for the congregation I serve in identifying needs in the congregation that we have not been able to meet in our current staffing configuration. The feedback we received from the focus groups has helped us to push forward with additional staff to meet identified needs.

Seeking quality feedback takes time, energy, and intention, but it stands as one of the pillars that needs to be constructed for an effective long-term pastorate.

Pillar # 5: Sustaining Growth—Seeking Depth

Certainly all of the pillars just identified are important and necessary for long-term pastorates to be effective. But this final pillar is both the key to long pastorates and, perhaps, the most difficult to maintain. The key to a pastor sustaining a growing edge in ministry is spiritual deepening and growth.

Those outside the clergy ranks may think that this would be easy for a pastor to do. After all, isn't this what we offer our parishioners through our preaching and teaching? The reality is, however, that we clergy-types have to work at this and that is why it is listed as a pillar.

The Three Poles (and Pulls) for a Parish Pastor

There are three poles that every parish pastor must strive to keep in balance: *ministry*, *family/community*, and *spiritual formation*. We have already discussed how ministry, both as a calling and a profession, will take every ounce of energy, every second of time, and every moment of thought we can give it. And that can lead to burnout, as we discussed before. Keeping these poles, which certainly pull and tug at us, in balance can go a long way in avoiding that problem.

Certainly the pull of family is understood. It is the source of our primary relationship where we know love, forgiveness, and grace in its fullest for our lives. Clergy spouses and children know the effect of the pull of ministry as a pastor spends countless hours and nights at meetings, counseling, or running to answer someone's call. Pastors expect the family to understand when evenings are interrupted or vacations postponed or shortened, but even that understanding has its limits. Therefore, pastors must seek to balance time, energy, and commitments to family. The family should not be called upon to always make the sacrifice.

The "Interior Life" of the Pastor

But there is a third pole that needs attention—the spiritual life of the pastor. Laypeople not only do not understand why a pastor needs to work at this since it is something that the pastor does professionally, they also offer little support to the pastor in meeting this need.

No one can tend to the interior life of the pastor but the pastor him- or herself. The pull of ministry, where there are spiritual tasks to do, complicates all this. So, we spend time reading scripture in preparation to preach or teach, rather than to feed our interior life. We work to write prayers for the gathered community in worship that express their joys and concerns and forget how to identify and pray for our own needs. We spend energy listening to others and caring for them as best we can and neglect to listen to our own souls. The agenda of the next meeting takes precedence over the voice crying in our hearts.

The Loss of the Three Basic Spiritual Disciplines of Laypeople

Laypeople enjoy three basic forms of spirituality: scripture, prayer, and worship. When a pastor becomes ordained, there is the danger of losing all three of those. Scripture can become preparation, prayer can become a task, and worship can become performance.

Since I have already touched on scripture and prayer, let me say a word about worship and its potential loss for us. For a parish pastor, worship is the most visible and most important thing we do. Done well, it takes planning, coordination, study, and effort. It means paying attention to detail, cooperating with other staff or laypersons with worship responsibilities, and expending lots of energy. It is often the point of first contact with new people and is, therefore, critical to any growth in membership. It requires of us the preparation of prayers, the training of all kinds of worship assistants from greeters and ushers to acolytes and altar guild members, and the discipline of regular sermon preparation.

And when all is prepared, Sunday or Saturday rolls around, and we stand before the congregation ready to execute all the effort, our question becomes, How do we worship? How do we worship when worship is a major responsibility we feel, know, and own?

Here is where I think being in a staff situation has a decided advantage. On a staff, a pastor does not have to have all the responsibility all the time. On a staff, a pastor can hear and appropriate the prayers of others. On a staff, the pastor can share the responsibility for training the hosts of volunteers needed. And on a staff, a pastor can have the Word preached to him- or herself from time to time.

Staff ministries have their share of serious issues that need to be addressed, but one of the clear blessings is in the area of worship. And the blessing has more to do with having the opportunity to be a worshiping person rather than being a pastor who is simply freed from having to preach every week.

Ideas for Spiritual Growth and Deepening

The issue of spiritual growth for pastors has received renewed emphasis lately, and not just in books addressed to pastors on the subject. There seems to be a growing enlightenment in seminaries these days about the need to help develop pastors who are not only aware of their need for spiritual growth but also to help them develop disciplines for that growth. Since more in-depth materials are available, I will simply offer a bulleted list of ideas for pastors to consider in the development of this important pillar of sustaining a growing edge for ministry and seeking depth:

- *Meditation*: Seek to be intentional about being in the presence of God on a regular and disciplined way.
- *Journaling*: Reflect on your spiritual journey by giving words to the pilgrimage of faith.
- *Using a Spiritual Director*: Find someone who can be a pastor to you and hold you accountable for your spiritual journey.
- *Fasting*: Since it is hard to be in touch with spiritual hunger when we live in a satisfied state, this discipline can help us deepen prayer and faith life with regular practice. There is debate about whether fasting is a healthy practice or not; my experience is fasting done properly deepens spiritual life.
- *Pilgrimages*: This is often a good way to start a sabbatical. My first and only trip to the Holy Land was one of the most remarkable experiences of my life. Every pastor should take at least one trip, although safety conditions now are a major concern.
- *Kinesthetic Spirituality*: Did you know that such practices as running, walking, swimming, and biking can be spiritual exercises?

The Value of a Sabbatical Leave

All of the ideas just mentioned take discipline and intention, and the pull of the ministry and family poles can sidetrack the best of our efforts. There is value, however, in an extended time away from the demands of ministry that will nourish our interior life and refresh our souls. A sabbatical leave offers a wonderful opportunity to find our centers again and to be reminded of what is truly important and real in our lives. It can be a time to rethink our priorities or to develop a new interest. It can be a time to listen to God in ways we do not allow amid the expectations that are placed upon us. It can offer a place to be a child of God and not a pastor with a dozen things to do or think about. It can help us feel at home again in our own skins.

The development of a sabbatical policy for all staff should be undertaken early in a ministry if there is not such a policy in place. This will allow time for the education of the congregation as to why such an extended time away is both important and necessary for the health of their pastor. It will also seem less self-serving if it is developed before it is needed and includes all the members of the staff with program responsibilities.

❖   ❖   ❖

This was a long chapter to wade through, but these five pillars are at the center of much of the research on effective long-term pastorates. There is much more that could be said to help define and amplify each pillar, but I think enough has been said so that it is clear why each pillar is needed and what that pillar supports.

There is one issue that needs more attention than we could give it in this chapter: the issue of support for clergy. How do we develop a support system that can nurture, challenge, and enrich us? The next chapter looks at this important and sometimes neglected issue.

CHAPTER 6

Beyond the Walls

Developing Support Systems

Meet Jim. He graduated from one of his denomination's seminaries. He fulfilled all the required courses in the four disciplines that tend to govern religious academic institutions these days—namely, biblical studies, church history, systematic theology, and practical theology. He completed chaplaincy work at a hospital one summer and learned a lot about himself in that role. He also completed a required internship in a congregational setting where he put on the title of "pastor," doing the work of one who wears such a title under the supervision, mentoring, and critique of that parish's pastor.

Through it all, Jim had grown and excelled. He was bright, so the academics, although challenging, were what he had expected. His year's internship was another period of growing and learning. He was fortunate to serve with, not under, a pastor who had served faithfully in ministry for many years and who had obviously established a loving and trusting relationship with a parish. He was directive without being controlling and definitive without being smug. Jim was treated like a colleague in ministry and not like a "junior lackey."

Like most pastors, Jim's models for ministry grew out of his long-time relationships in his home church and in his denomination. The pastor he knew at his hometown church had been there through most of Jim's growing-up years. Although not the best preacher in the world, he was nevertheless beloved by the members of the congregation to whom he had given tireless and selfless devotion.

At the seminary, Jim had learned the scholastic side of ministry from some of the best in their disciplines. His systematics professor had always told the students that they were to be, above all else, "the theologian-in-residence" in their parishes. He believed that to be truth. His internship pastor was another model of dedication, commitment, and compassion.

He worked long hours in responding to the needs of his flock, always looking for ways to present the gospel in new and fresh ways.

How do you like Jim so far? He has had the academic and pastoral training that is required and has done very well in all of his educational settings. From all the reports, he has both the head and the heart to be an effective pastor. He is bright, competent, compassionate, mature, dedicated, and now, equipped. The committee of his denomination responsible for approving candidates for ordination, called the Committee of Our Denomination Responsible for Approving Candidates for Ordination, or CRDRACO for short, has given him the stamp of approval.

Let us fast-forward the story a bit. Jim is in his first call and has very quickly discovered that there are things about parish ministry that were not taught in seminary—lots of things; one of the main ones being how to deal with difficult situations like the ghost of the former pastor still hovering around. It seems that Jim's leadership style is being called into question at every turn. "He is not like Pastor _____." "Pastor _____ would have done it this way." "Why can't you be more like our beloved Pastor _____?"

The pain of the situation caused sleepless nights and self-doubt. The whole thing hit a boiling point when, during a congregational meeting, someone asked why Jim was called to be a pastor to their parish since he obviously had little skills that they needed. The words hurt like nothing Jim had ever experienced before. Nothing during his seminary training had prepared him for how to handle the pain and range of emotions that pain was causing. His wife was a good listener, but the pain was her pain, too, and Jim was afraid that she would turn bitter and resentful toward the congregation. How should he handle himself? What could he do that would help him deal with his growing disillusionment about parish ministry? Why hadn't anyone prepared him for this kind of situation?

Is this a true story? Well, Jim was fictitious, but the story certainly was not; just overstated and overdrawn to make a point. The educational model for preparing persons for ministry has gone through a number of changes over the last two decades. Most denominations have added some form of hospital or clinical training. Many have required some form of supervised internship of varying lengths to give ministers-in-training a sense of the "real" world of parish ministry. We have done an excellent job in teaching seminarians how to exegete passages of scripture, how to interpret both the First and Second Testaments, how to think theologically, how to counsel persons who come to us in various forms of need, how to preach, how to teach, and even, in some more astute seminaries, how to be a leader.

In short, we have taught Jim to stand on his own, to be a competent pastor for a congregation who would call him, and to do all those tasks necessary to be an effective pastor with and for his people. There is just one problem with this model—we have neglected to show him one of the key pillars discussed in the last chapter: namely, how to take care of himself by developing support systems that would help him to stay healthy.

Remaking the Lone Ranger Image

There is no doubt that our denominational seminaries do the best job they know how to do in educating students in the academic disciplines necessary to be parish pastors. Someone has said that if you wanted to train a person completely for ministry it would take a lifetime, and there is a measure of truth to that. Although, from the standpoint of those of us who have served for years in this calling, there are some obvious holes in that education as observed (like courses on administration and leadership), seminaries do what the church asks them to do—namely, educate. Our denominations have also put into place opportunities for candidates to have their calls and their gifts for ministry tested and observed.

But in and through all of this, one gets the underlying sense of the pastor being trained to be the Lone Ranger out there in the world. The three C's of cooperation, collegiality, and care for one another seem to be overlooked in the rush of three or four years of intensive preparation. Our Lone Rangers have been prepared well for life in the parish. We are taught to do it all, do it well, and be the pillar of leadership and strength that congregations are looking for.

The problem is (if we can stay with this metaphor for a moment longer) the Lone Ranger gets lonely. Moreover, unless Jim had a model of ministry to observe that was honest about that fact and he had learned how to deal with the issue, his seminary education taught him neither the reality of ministry nor any healthy ways to cope with that reality.

It is time for our systems of theological education—including the seminaries of our denominations and the Committees of Our Denominations Responsible for Approving Candidates for Ordination—to see that the current model they propose for seminarians to examine has a missing leg. For me, that leg has been building a network of supportive colleagues who have been there to comfort, guide, and challenge me during critical times in the life of my ministry.

This is an issue of such importance that I have chosen to give it a chapter of its own. I do not remember being told, encouraged, or taught to develop a support system while traveling through seminary. I do not recall anyone from my judicatory ever suggesting it. My models for ministry all seemed to be self-sufficient, strong, competent, and committed people who did not appear to need or have anyone to support them. In other words, no one modeled or showed me how the Lone Ranger deals with the "lone" part of the office.

An aside is in order here. In my desire to be inclusive regarding examples, Jim originally was Mary. Three different people, in reading the story for editing purposes, commented to me that the illustration would probably work better in the male gender, since common wisdom says that women clergy are more likely either to form a support system or bring one from other dimensions of their lives prior to entering ministry. There is not enough time for the purposes of this book to explore that folk wisdom. So, Jim it is, with a nod or two to the Marys who find themselves in need of support and care from other clergy.

Being Intentional about Creating a Support System

Since it seems that no one has ever taught us to develop a support system, the responsibility for doing so rests with us, the pastors who need one. If our health and growth are important for us personally and professionally, then developing some sort of support system becomes crucial. And, since it will not simply happen for us, we need to take some initiative.

Some have noted that most clergy support groups do not function well because of two interrelated factors. First, unless there is a facilitator (more on that in a moment), there will probably be no strong leadership at the center of the group. That leadership is what helps hold the group together over a period of time. Second, because there is no leadership, no trust develops, and with no trust, there is no sharing. How can there be any support if we hold all the joys and sorrows, all the highs and lows, inside and do not share them with those in the group?

Therefore, a facilitator needs to be chosen, someone "outside" the group, if you will. This facilitator will function to keep the dialogue and discussion focused, open, honest, and real. The facilitator will keep the extroverts in the group from dominating all the airtime and encourage the introverts to share their thoughts, concerns, and struggles. It is also a good idea to pay this facilitator for his or her services. By doing so, there is more ownership of the role by all concerned. There is also a sense of investment in the process when money is exchanged.

The intentional formation of a support group should be done with care. The size of the group should probably not be over eight people, with six being optimum. People invited to be part of the group should make a commitment for a given period of time and should pledge to make the group meetings a priority. If someone cannot commit to regular meetings, she or he should not consider being a part of the group until such time as they can commit to attending regularly.

Going "Beyond the Walls"

The quality of support in such a clergy support group really comes from the fact that only peers can ever really know and understand the issues of other pastors, even pastors from other faith traditions (more on that in a moment). This is why it is important to go "beyond the walls" of our churches to find such support. Even the most informed and knowledgeable members of our parishes do not know, nor can we expect them to know, the range of emotions and the depth of feelings that go with the office of pastor. They certainly can empathize, but not in the same way that other pastors who know the struggles and joys firsthand can.

Right after attending the Alban Institute seminar on long-term pastorates with a neighboring colleague, the two of us decided to form a support group of our peers. Although we were from different faith traditions, we thought the support we could get from one another and from others in our community would be helpful and healthful. So, we got together and asked a pastoral counselor that we knew and trusted to be our facilitator. She agreed and together we brainstormed pastors in the immediate area whom we thought would contribute and benefit from such a group. We wanted no "prima donnas," persons whom we did not feel we could trust in the sharing process or pastors who knew all the answers to everyone else's problems. Like it or not, we are political animals, and we did not want someone whom we did not trust with the honest sharings we hoped would be part of the group experience.

We also sought to have some balance in the group between male and female clergy, between those new to the community and those who had been here for some time, between those pastors who were in senior positions and those who were associates or assistants, and between various faith traditions. What we ended up with was a group of six clergy plus a facilitator that was balanced in gender, tenure, position, and denomination. And, surprisingly, we stayed together as a group for almost four years, meeting twice a month for two-hour sessions.

A word may be in order about the mixture of those in different ministry offices, that is, senior pastors and associate or assistant pastors. Over the last 10 years, I have been involved in the support group mentioned above and then in one that I helped form made up of only senior pastors of large churches in my denomination. Both support groups were helpful to me for different reasons. In the first group mentioned in the preceding paragraph, the mixture of pastors of both genders and positions added a dynamic to the sharing that was missing from the later group of all male senior pastors. Luckily, the senior pastor support group was made up of trusted colleagues who were willing to share and leave their egos at the door. But there was a different level of sharing when the mix of the group was more diverse. I learned, for instance, that males and females really do think differently. Maybe I'm dense, but it took me a long time to figure that out, but the group was helpful in that learning. There were times when one of the female clergy would share something and I would have to ask the facilitator to translate that into language I could understand. There was no put-down intended and, after we laughed about it, we all learned from such experiences. The other issue of major learning had to do with staff dynamics and the sharing of those who were in associate or assistant positions. Interpersonal issues in staffs are sometimes the most difficult to deal with. Having persons in the group from different perspectives of the issues was helpful for all of us.

So, we need to be intentional in forming support groups. What are the goals of such a group? What do we see as the life span of the group? Where would it be "safe" to meet? Can those who said they would participate commit to the time and the goals? Will everyone commit to the confidentiality of the sharing? Can egos that go with positions be left at the door so that trust and openness can develop? Can we go "beyond the walls" of the denomination so that our worlds can be expanded a bit? These are some of the issues involved in being intentional about forming a support group.

Here is a short list of suggestions for how a clergy support group might operate:

- Develop a covenant, either verbal or written, that includes:
  a. Attendance at meetings and making them a priority on one's schedule
  b. Confidentiality
  c. An initial 9-12 month commitment, renegotiated at the end of that initial period
  d. New persons are made part of the group by invitation only and by agreement with all in the current group
- Plan for meetings every other week or once a month at the most, with summers off
- Agree to meet for 1½–2 hours each time
- Have a paid facilitator (more on that later)
- Meet at a setting where everyone feels safe and a climate of hospitality can be established
- Begin with an open format where anyone can share whatever is on her or his mind or heart
- Negotiate carry-over agenda items at the end of the meeting for the next time
- Agree that no one should dominate the group discussion and that everyone should be heard and respected

Ways the Judicatory Can Help

It seems to me that our judicatories are becoming more proactive in regard to support of their pastors. In many places first-call pastors serving in those early critical years of ministry are being assigned mentors, that is, pastors with some years of experience and knowledge to share those first steps in ministry. Pastoral associations based on geography can help establish relationships that are mutually supportive and encouraging. The problem, as all of us know who have served in ministry and been a part of such associations, is that egos (in other words, sin) and trust issues are very much a part of such groups. Although healthy relationships of trust can develop, they need to be intentionally developed by any pastor because they are not the norm among pastoral groups. The pastoral groups of which

I have been a part have normally been too large for any degree of deep trust to develop and made up of people who come to such meetings with diverse and often-conflicting agendas. Some pastors come for the collegiality, others to share information; some want the group to be a mini-seminar on the latest theological fad, while others want the chance to share what hurts with those who may know something about that hurt. With conflicting agendas and large groups such meetings often become frustrating events, easily avoided with more pressing items on our agendas.

Judicatories can do two, maybe three, things to help develop support systems for clergy. First, bishops and conference pastors can be on the lookout for those pastors who they think would benefit from such a support group. Their first clue to such a person might be someone who is going through a particularly difficult time and could benefit from regular support of fellow pastors. An encouraging word to such a pastor about forming a support network for her- or himself and then some suggestions about how to do that and who to ask to be a part of the group would be in order. The problem is that when we are hurting over an issue, all our energy goes into dealing with that hurt and we may not have the focus to create such a helpful support group at that time. It is better to create such a group when we can do so without the pressure of a conflict or painful issue sapping our energies. The judicatories can help by encouraging such groups to be formed.

Second, since it is helpful to have a paid facilitator in support groups, someone who sits somewhat outside the group and helps keep focus, the judicatories can assist by recommending counselors and facilitators they know and trust who could serve in that role. We will examine what to look for in a facilitator in a moment.

And finally, third (a maybe third, but one to consider nonetheless), judicatory officials can network with their counterparts in other denominations to encourage support groups that are pan-denominational. Resource lists of good facilitators could be shared and those who wish to form a support system could be put in touch with those with similar needs from other church families.

While I recognize the difficulties with this last suggestion, much can be said in its favor. The most effective support group I was ever a part of was multidenominational by intention. Although I cannot universalize that experience and say that such a group is the only way to go in developing a support group, consider these two factors when contemplating the formation of such a diverse group.

First, safety and trust can develop where there are fewer political issues among the participants. We all know that it is difficult to share personal issues with someone who has the potential of using that information in ways that would violate trust. Going outside of our own denominational walls reduces that risk somewhat. Pastors who are not part of our system of governance probably can not affect us in that system like those who are politically a part of it.

Second, on a more positive note, the inclusion of pastors from other traditions means that we can learn more about one another. One of the things we discover is that we are more similar in terms of the issues that affect us than we imagined. Pastoral hurts cross denominational lines in their content and it is often helpful and supportive just to learn that we are not alone in our struggles. We also have the added benefit of learning how others relate their theologies to their practices.

What to Look for in a Facilitator

A group facilitator of a support system should have three qualities. First, they need to be *competent*. They need to understand, appreciate, and have experience in group dynamics and interpersonal relationships. It is their task to engage all the participants in the group over time, even the extreme introverts. It is also their role to keep the discussion focused and on track. They need to know when to insert themselves into the sharing and when to sit back to listen and observe. And their insertions into the discussion should not only be timely, but with the precision of a surgeon, with just the right question that might move the sharing into deeper and more painful waters.

Second, the facilitator needs to be *sensitive*. We clergy types are pretty good at covering our struggles on a day-to-day basis. We smile outside with deep pain under our eyes. A sensitive and alert facilitator can see through such defenses and might help us move that pain out into the open where other pastoral strugglers can offer their healing and supportive words.

Finally, a facilitator must be *a safe person* for us. We must be able to trust them with ourselves. For that reason, it is good to find a person who is not a part of our judicatory, political system. If a facilitator is viewed as a part of the system, we are less likely to have the trust to share openly and honestly for fear that what we say may come back later to haunt us. As a result, members will not build trust among themselves, and we already know what happens when there is no trust in a group.

The qualities just mentioned are important to keep in mind, but there is another factor to consider in finding a good facilitator. I personally think that the facilitator should be a pastor, one who has known on a first-hand basis the struggles we will share. There is something about having someone who has been there that bridges any credibility gap and that helps us to move into trust relationships in a faster way. Someone who has "been there" and "done that" with the qualities mentioned before will have a different perspective than one who knows about the issues second-hand or through academics.

❖ ❖ ❖

Time to move on to the number one issue that all of us face in pastoral ministry—namely, people issues. If we are going to survive over the long haul we need to practice and nurture some basic principles of dealing with people, both volunteers and staff.

CHAPTER 7

Where Two or Three Gather
Supervising and Nurturing Church Staffs and Volunteers

Parish ministry is first and foremost about the proclamation of a particular message. Our preaching and teaching all center around an articulated theology that has been formulated over the years by our faith tradition. This theology is learned, passed down over decades of refinement, and now becomes the working theology we seek to pass on to those in our care. So far, so good.

Then we discover that the main problems facing us in any parish do not center on theology. After all that seminary preparation in which we learned to become the "theologian-in-residence," we discover that the biggest issues we face are often over seemingly trivial matters, like whether to pass the peace during flu season or the use of a common cup for communion. And it probably does not take long for us to discover that when two or three gather, according to the biblical injunction, there can and will be issues to face. As I used to say in my first parish where folks were prone to fight about everything, "where two or three gather, there will be four strong differences of opinion!"

So, if any of us intend to stay in parish ministry beyond the first sunset, and especially if we intend to stay in a parish for the long haul, it is important to consider the "people" issues of ministry, for those issues are the ones that rub against us most often. In order for ministry to occur in any setting, regardless of size of congregation, there must be leadership that understands and appreciates the dynamics of interrelationships. Even more importantly, though, for ministry to be done well, leadership must be given in the areas of supervision of staff and/or volunteers and the nurturing of those with whom we partner in ministry.

Developing a Leadership Edge:
Understanding Both Efficiency and Effectiveness

Management guru Peter Drucker was not the first to articulate the difference between efficiency and effectiveness, but he was the first to voice it clearly for modern audiences. He makes the distinction between the two as follows: efficiency is "getting things done right," while effectiveness is "getting the right things done." The first deals with *how* things are done and the other with *what* is done and in what order. Both are important in any leadership role. In terms of effectiveness, it is the leader of any organization who helps determine the path. In a congregational setting, the pastor is the one who helps formulate the mission and vision of that parish, and then gives voice to it. In terms of efficiency, it is again the leader who determines how things get done in any organization. In a parish setting, it is the pastor who sets the tone for the work of the parish, a work in which all are encouraged to participate.

Let me reiterate one minor example of the latter issue. When I came to my present call, I soon discovered a congregation that, in my terms, was "pitched in a minor key." There was so much behind-the-scenes grumbling and fussing that I determined that the first order of business as the new pastor was to change the way we worked, played, worshiped, and talked with one another. Before we could begin to be effective in our ministry, we needed to learn to do things right, which included how we listened to and treated one another. So, I decreed, rather tight-fistedly, that any complaints would be dealt with only if the complainer would come forward and own the issue, and then agree to be part of the solution. Grumbling went underground for a time, but then, when there was no reward for it, soon diminished considerably. Only then could we concentrate on the issues that we needed to work on, like staffing and articulating our mission.

Interlink Consultants, Ltd., who conduct seminars around the country for pastors, have identified five "Characteristics of Effectiveness"[1] in leaders. These characteristics are worth examining and commenting upon because they directly relate to how we supervise and support our volunteers and staffs. These are the characteristics that set the stage for us in our working relationships in the parish, and they include:

- *Knowing where we are going.* Our parishioners and, in the case of being a senior member of a staff, our staff members assume that we know where we are going. This is one of the trademarks of effective leadership and it helps develop trust in that leadership if people know that we know what we are about and where we are going.

- *Focusing on outward contributions.* How do we measure the work of ministry? What are the ways we know that the work we are called to do is being done? How can we quantify the day-to-day life of the parish? For there to be any discernible growth, there must be a way to measure that growth.

- *Building on strengths.* Smart, effective leaders surround themselves with people who have strengths different from their own. They know that if they are going to be effective, they need to have good people doing the tasks that they have neither the heart nor the gifts to do themselves. This is one of the "irrefutable" laws of leadership as identified by pastor and management guru John C. Maxwell. He called it "The Law of the Inner Circle."[2] "Think of any highly effective leader," he writes, "and you will find someone who surrounded himself with a strong inner circle."[3]

- *Concentrating on a few major areas.* Effective leaders know their own strengths and build on them. Leaders do not have to do it all and certainly pastors cannot. It is simply good stewardship to use well the gifts God has given us and to encourage others to do the same.

- *Making effective decisions.* The leader of any organization is known by the decisions she or he makes. Prioritizing the tasks of ministry is a good way to make effective decisions about what needs doing. Over time in a parish, those priorities change and we must change with them. It has been said that sometimes it is better to make a wrong decision than no decision. This is all about being effective as persons called into leadership positions.

Learning the Art of Delegating

Delegation is defined as sharing a portion of our responsibility and authority with others in order to accomplish more productive work. Effective leaders know the importance of delegation and clear communication is the key to effective delegating.

In a church setting, there is much that obviously needs to be delegated. Some of that delegating goes to staff, if the congregation is large enough, but much of it goes to laypersons. We encourage people to use the gifts God has given them in service to their God, to one another, and to the world. Shared ministry means that all of us take a part in it. With responsibility come ownership and a stake in what is happening. Encouraging the talents of all to serve the greater good is the best stewardship we can have.

Interlink Consultants has identified a four-step process in delegating:[4]

1. *Select*: Match the skills of people with the identified needs; get the right persons for the jobs;
2. *Communicate*: This involves an eight-step formula: what, when, how many, how well, who, where, how much, and why; we communicate all we know about what we are asking someone to commit to;
3. *Train/Coach*: It is important to make sure that people know how to do the job we are asking them to do; sometimes this is done through regular supervision, or mentoring, or by example; and,
4. *Follow Up*: This process allows for two things to happen:
   (*a*) it shows support and lets the person know you care about what they are doing; and
   (*b*) it makes sure that the person is on the right track with the job, that you gave clear communication, and that the person understood it.

Because burnout is such a real danger in ministry, learning the art of delegating is crucial in both expanding the breadth of ministry and keeping us from over-committing. I know of a pastor who left each of his first three parishes after about three or four years because he was such an idea person that he would initiate one new ministry opportunity after another. The problem was, he never learned to delegate and soon had too many balls in the air to juggle. The only solution, at least in his mind, was to leave.

The Role of Equipping Laity

This brings us to an important and often neglected role of clergy—equipping the laity for service in the church and the world. Many of us know the biblical text: "The gifts he [God] gave were that some would be apostles, some prophets, some evangelists, some pastors and teachers, to equip the saints for the work of ministry, for building up the body of Christ" (Ephesians 4:11-12). In their important book *The Equipping Pastor*, pastoral theologians

Paul Stevens and Phil Collins set out to understand the role of the pastor in regard to this biblical injunction, putting this role into the context of a systems approach to understanding congregational leadership. They begin by explaining the role of pastors-teachers: They "were given to the church to equip the saints to do ministry. . . . The equipping pastor is not merely one who gets the lay people to assist her or him. No, the equipping pastor assists the people to fulfill their own ministry, a much greater thing."[5]

Church consultant Norman Shawchuck has given us a very simple definition of leadership: "Leadership is the ability and the activity of influencing people and of shaping their behavior."[6] To lead, as I have suggested before, is to possess a vision and to carry responsibility for an organization's program and purpose. But that is never done alone or in a vacuum. Being an effective leader requires an understanding of how one's leadership behavior affects other people. The leader must always consider the behavior of individual group members and the situations in which these people carry out their work. Anytime someone attempts to influence or persuade the behavior of another person or group, regardless of the reason, he or she is exercising leadership. This means, of course, that the pastor is obviously only one of the leaders of the church.

Part of our role as pastors is to cultivate a spirit of interdependence among and with the people we serve. This interdependence holds in tension two essential dimensions of the church: unity or togetherness and the existence and function of each member of the church, that is, diversity. A healthy leader finds ways to cultivate this interdependence so that not only are individuals served, but the body is served as well.

There is not enough time for the purposes of this book to explore this important area of equipping the saints. Stevens and Collins have done a masterful job in their book and I commend it to you. However, let me summarize just a few of their points in order to encourage your further exploration:

- Equipping is essentially a relational, rather than a programmatic ministry. The role of equipping the saints involves building the people of God first and foremost.
- We, as leaders, have the unique challenge of building unity among the people of God but without evoking autonomy. This means we encourage people to remain connected with one another while at the same time we help them to define themselves and their own ministries based on their gifts, rather than merely asking them to assist us in our ministry.

- Leadership is always the starting point for healthy, shared ministry. We need to teach and model interdependence and, even more difficult for some of us, allow others to minister *to* us.
- One of the ways that leaders model this interdependence is by clearly defining themselves, their gifts, talents, and energies, and encouraging others to do the same. We do this in the context of the community of faith with the result that our shared visions become the starting point for God to open each of us to new ways of seeing.
- Equipping pastors are always looking for giftedness in the community of faith and naming those gifts as they are recognized. In this way we model how to affirm the contributions of all members of the household of faith in a way that builds up each one, affirming our unity amid the wonderful diversity God has given us.[7]

Situational Leadership and Its Lessons

Stevens and Collins in their book rely on the time-tested two-dimensional view of leadership developed by social scientists Robert Blake and Jane Mouton.[8] In this view, a person's style of leadership is either concerned for people or concerned for task or production. They contend that there is no biblical or theological support for one style of leadership over another and that there is no one style that is intrinsically better at equipping the saints for service than the other. Then, they conclude their discussion with these insightful comments: "We are convinced that effective equipping of the saints requires a leader whose style is matched to the congregation."[9]

We need to take that last statement and expand it somewhat. Stevens and Collins talk about matching a pastor's leadership style to a congregation as a systemic unit. While it is true that we need to relate to the organization, the body, of the congregation, what about how we relate to those individual members, both staff and volunteers, with whom we share ministry?

Kenneth Blanchard and Paul Hersey have developed a helpful model of leadership that takes into account that not every person needs to be nor should be supervised and nurtured in the same way. Their model, known as "Situational Leadership" has been widely read and used both in business, professional, and church circles. Blanchard has condensed the theory in his little book (co-authored by Patricia Zigarmi and Drea Zigarmi), *Leadership and the One-Minute Manager*.[10]

Blanchard and Hersey contend that all managers, whatever the circumstances of the work arena, need to learn to be flexible in the style of leadership they use as they seek to use their authority and power to accomplish a task. The four styles, discussed below, actually consist of different combinations of two basic leadership behaviors: directive behavior and supportive behavior. *Directive behavior* can be defined by the verbs *structure, organize, teach,* and *supervise,* while *supportive* behavior is described by the verbs *praise, listen, ask, explain,* and *facilitate.* What is important to keep in mind in understanding this model is that no one leadership style is always right all the time. As Blanchard's book puts it, "There is nothing so unequal as the equal treatment of unequals."[11]

So, we, as pastors, need to learn to deal with people according to their needs for supervision and support. The four leadership styles identified by situational leadership are:

- "*Style 1: Directing.* The leader provides specific direction and closely monitors task accomplishment." This style is appropriate when a decision has to be made quickly, the stakes are high, or when we are dealing with inexperienced people.
- "*Style 2: Coaching.* The leader continues to direct and closely monitor task accomplishment, but also explains decisions, solicits suggestions, and supports progress." This style combines both direction and support and works best when disillusionment has set in for the one asked to do a task.
- "*Style 3: Supporting.* The leader facilitates and supports people's efforts toward task accomplishment and shares responsibility for decision making with them." It is a style that is used when there is a competent or experienced person who lacks confidence. This is actually the strongest leadership style in a healthy congregation.
- "*Style 4: Delegating.* The leader turns over responsibility for decision making and problem solving to people." This style is appropriate for people who are self-reliant achievers—people who are both competent and committed. This style works best in a work environment where there are competent specialists who like one another.[12]

It is interesting to me, personally, that I actually learned this theory "in theory" about 10 years ago. Somehow it rolled off my back. Schooled and trained in the model of "being consistent means being dependable," I treated staff equally over a long period of time. I discovered the flaw in that approach when we called an inexperienced staff member and I continued to use the Supporting Style (my normal operating stance) when this person really needed me to be a Directing person. Frustration set in for me fairly quickly because I had high expectations and the congregation had high demands. The staff member became frustrated because it seemed that he could not accomplish what needed to be done.

Situational leadership is a good model for anyone who must work with others to accomplish mutually agreed-upon tasks. The effective leader is one who can read a situation and respond with the appropriate style. I commend the Blanchard and Zigarmi book as a brief introduction and a way to easily understand the concepts. It is highly readable with graphs and charts that are easy to grasp.

Appreciating the Gifts of Those Around Us

Recognizing the validity of the theory just presented and the two poles of directing and supporting, let me add a personal word or two about the supporting side of that equation. One of our basic human needs is to be needed and appreciated. The worst thing we can ever do in marriage is to take our partner for granted. Well, the same could be applied to relationships in general and to life in the church in particular. As a pastor, we dare not take for granted the gifts of time and talent of those who are part of the ministry of that church. And it is equally as important to find ways of showing appreciation for the efforts of those who are paid to work within the church as it is to appreciate those who volunteer their time and energies.

So, here is a brief list of ways to appreciate, recognize, and support the gifts of those around us:

- Keep a note card in your hymnal or prayer book each week and as you look over the congregation, write down the names of those who would appreciate a note. And then,
- Write notes thanking people for their efforts and time. Write lots of notes, all the time. Write a few notes each week. It goes a long way to show your acknowledgement and appreciation of their gifts. This includes to staff, as well.
- Acknowledge the work of members of the church on any given project in your church bulletin or newsletter.

- Have someone who can write articles for the local newspaper and highlight projects to publicize, always giving acknowledgement to those who are putting forth the effort.
- Have a banquet once or twice a year to honor those who give of their time and efforts.
- Take staff out to lunch or dinner on occasion to thank them for a particularly fine job on a task or mission.
- Model this appreciation style of ministry so that staff or leaders within the congregation will also take the time to thank, acknowledge, and show support of others.
- Have a Volunteer Appreciation Sunday and print all the names of those who use their time and talents. If you serve a large church, consider doing this for specific projects and having a few of these Sundays a year.
- Bulletin boards that highlight ministries within the congregation can also be used to mention and show appreciation for the gifts of those who participate.
- For extraordinary service, you may consider a special gift. If someone has served for years and years and has finally decided to "retire," why not give them a gift? My own mother taught third-grade Sunday school for 35 years, without summers off. When she finally retired, my home congregation did two things: They gave her a gift Bible (I actually thought that was a tad late. Why not give teachers good Bibles early in their tenure?) and they elected her to the congregation council (which I thought was cruel and unusual punishment!). My point, I think, is made—somehow acknowledge long, excellent, and faithful service.
- Always, always find time to thank someone in person when it is possible. A phone call, a visit, or a few words in the narthex after services goes a long way to show that you care about someone and appreciate what they have done.

Serving in a church for a long time takes management skills that few of us were ever taught in seminary. But learning to supervise and support staff and volunteers is an important skill to learn if our ministry is to grow and be healthy and effective.

Chapter 8

Within the Walls
Creating a Congregational Climate for the Long Haul

Although primarily addressing the issue of staffing for large churches, church consultant Lyle Schaller raises the issues of a long pastorate for congregational growth: "While there is no evidence to prove that either long pastorates or expansion of the program staff will produce numerical growth in a church, there is very persuasive evidence that suggests it is rare to find a growing congregation that has sustained its growth over a long period of time that has not had the benefits of both long pastorates and an adequate program staff."[1] His point is, for a church to grow and (we assume) be healthy—since nonhealthy churches rarely grow—it is important to the congregation that a long pastorate is encouraged, supported, and sustained.

In fact, of the six advantages, or potential advantages, of long-term pastorates as discovered by the Alban Institute in their research, four of the advantages benefit both the pastor and the congregation. The most important of the advantages, as it pertains to the congregation, is this: "There is a greater continuity and stability of leadership and program in a long-term pastorate, which makes possible things which are not possible in a short-term pastorate."[2]

Certainly there are disadvantages to the congregation for long pastorates. But the Alban research also concluded that "Virtually all the disadvantages of a long-tenured pastorate can be surmounted, yet few of the advantages are available to clergy who remain in a congregation for only a short period of time."[3] By extension, since four of the advantages mentioned previously also are advantages to a congregation, it seems obvious that a congregation should strive to create a climate for the long haul.

The question, therefore, becomes, How? How does a congregation develop such a climate? Are there certain things a congregation can do to help nurture and support such a long-term relationship? How can the pastor and congregation grow up together? It seems to me that there are a few ways to create such a climate.

What Congregations Need to Hear

Perhaps the best place to begin is with those things a congregation needs to hear and learn early on in a pastorate. These words are probably best spoken by someone outside of the church, like a judicatory official, who speaks with some knowledge, authority, experience, and wisdom that the congregation can respect. What these words do is begin to provide an atmosphere where relationships of trust and confidence in a pastor can start to grow. Good climate, remember, helps things grow.

"This is not your parents' church."

In settings where there are more nuclear families than extended families, this is certainly not an issue. But where there are multiple generations worshiping in a setting for decades with accumulated histories of involvement, someone needs to gently remind everyone that "this is not your parents', or grandparents', church." Being tied too closely to a past, seeking to repeat its ministries, programs, and performance is a bind few new pastors are able to break. Yes, our histories are important and should be recognized, celebrated, and remembered—but not repeated. A pastor seeking to establish trust and relationships for the long haul will have to deal with the accumulated history of the parish and gently and persuasively move the church to the present.

"This is not your parents' pastor."

Needless to say, not all pastors are created equal. Gifts vary, as scripture reminds us, according to the Spirit. Therefore, every pastor brings gifts and talents that are different from their predecessor. Sometimes the congregation needs to remind herself that Pastor B, their current pastor, is not Pastor A, their beloved last pastor, who somehow was raised to sainthood upon her retirement. Since these first ideas are linked, it is a good idea to be clear in respecting the former pastor and his or her ministry, while at the same time being clear about the gifts we bring to the new setting. A healthy climate for the long haul can begin to be established on the clear gifts and talents we bring rather than trying to outdo the former pastor at what they did. Fighting the past is never a good idea. Learning from it, respecting it, and using it as a building tool, is.

"Let go, to embrace."

There is clearly a theme to these phrases and, when all is said and done, they probably all mean something of the same thing. For a congregation to move into a new future with a pastor who wants to serve and be faithful for the long haul, the past must somehow be the past. There is nothing worse for the beginning of a ministry than the long shadow of a former pastor that seems to be everywhere. And there is not a pastor alive who has not heard, no doubt during the first years of ministry in a setting, "But we've always done it that way!" The past certainly needs to inform our present, lest we repeat the mistakes previously made. However, being tied to a past in a changing world can hinder the present and obscure any new future that God may have in mind for a congregation. "Let go" means just that, so that everyone can "embrace" a new tomorrow. For a pastor seeking to serve for the long haul and a congregation who will benefit from such a relationship, such words need to be understood, acknowledged, and lived.

What Support Looks Like

Now that we have cleared the air, so to speak, and the atmosphere is right for a healthy relationship to develop between a pastor and a congregation, we move on to ask, "What does support look like in a congregational setting?" The following are ways that a congregation can show their support for a pastor and continue to enjoy a healthy relationship for the long haul:

1.   Develop a Pastor-Parish Relations Committee
Often called a mutual ministry committee in some church systems, this committee's sole function is to monitor the quality of the relationship between

the pastor and the congregation. Since this relationship is key to the ongoing life of a congregation and absolutely essential if there is to be a long-term pastorate, this committee holds an important function for the well being of both the pastor and congregation. This committee should not be the one to deal with personnel issues, such as job descriptions, performance evaluations, salary decisions, or personnel policies. A personnel committee should handle that role. Nor should the pastor-parish relations committee be the collection area for complaints from members of the congregation. An executive committee could handle such matters.

Rather, members of this committee should work to understand the pastor's perspective as well as her or his hopes, visions, and needs. In addition, they should seek to relate to the pastor's family in a way that offers ongoing support and encouragement. They should also seek to convey to the pastor their understanding of the congregation's life. They become, in a sense, the voice for the congregation as it responds to the hopes and perspective of their pastor. In this way, a safe environment can be developed for mutual and honest sharing. It is only when a congregation and a pastor truly understand one another that their relationship can stay healthy and all can grow and thrive.

A good resource for a congregation that does not have such a committee or that has one but wants to change the focus so that the committee is doing what it should be doing is Roy Oswald's video, *Why You Should Develop a Pastor-Parish Relations Committee.*[4] It comes with a leader guide so that the pastor can work with a board and congregational members to establish this important committee.

2. Maintain a Healthy Climate
One of the identified disadvantages of a long-term pastorate is that "as negative influences mount and begin to outweigh positive influences, a downward spiral may develop."[5] Therefore, maintaining a healthy climate is essential. While "negative attitudes can be catching,"[6] something of which we all know, the opposite can also be true—positive attitudes can become the norm.

There is nothing that can dampen the spirit of a group more than negativism, and a dampened spirit is a dispirited one. When ministry becomes drudgery, when going to the office is something we dread, when we'd rather have root canal work than attend a meeting at the church, when we have countless sleepless nights because of the dark clouds around us, no one can or will survive for very long.

A congregation that knows the value of a long-term pastorate will seek to create a climate where honesty, growth, challenge, and support are evident. I would also contend that this should be a place where fun is valued, where laughs are heard regularly, where the joy of life is experienced, and where people feel safe in being the persons God created in God's image. The church is the place where gifts are recognized, encouraged, and used for the sake of others. It is, or at least it should be, a place where people learn about forgiveness and reconciliation, two of the most important gifts the church gives the world. All of this maintains a climate where a pastor would want to stay, grow, and serve.

3. Financial Support

The last potential disadvantage for a long-term pastorate, as identified in the Alban study, is "a long pastorate may have some special reduction in benefits for the pastor and the pastor's family."[7] And one of those major reductions is that a pastor's financial situation may not improve in the same parish over many years.

Many judicatories have guidelines for the congregations in their geographical area to use in setting salary and benefits for their pastors. It would behoove a congregation to take those guidelines very seriously. One of the ways a congregation can concretely show a pastor that the members appreciate and support him or her is with adequate financial support. Certainly no one goes into the ministry expecting to get rich. But we do hope to live a reasonable life, compensated fairly for a difficult calling, and able to provide for our families, including sending children off to college. One of the things a congregation who wants to keep their pastor needs to do is to make it financially difficult to leave. That sounds rather crass, but the reality is that if a congregation treats a pastor fairly through adequate financial support, the chances of that pastor staying where the appreciation is shown is greatly increased.

One more word on this subject, addressed to judicatory officials. This is an area where many pastors need help. I once heard a statistic that over half of the congregations in our country where judicatories have compensation guidelines in place pay below those salary guidelines. When I started my first call almost 30 years ago, I was paid $2,000 more than my predecessor who served there for 15 years and was in his 50s when he had his heart attack. The church felt guilty about how they had treated him and his family, and well they should have. It was the judicatory official who set the stage for this new pastor to come in and be paid within guidelines and I appreciate his efforts. Similar work needs to be done, and forthrightly, throughout the church in this land. End of homily on this topic!

4. Encourage Strong Lay Leadership

Ministry has always been a partnership. Those called to Word and Sacrament ministry are set aside within the community of faith as trained leaders whose functions include the equipping of the saints for ministry, the guidance and oversight of the gifts of the fellowship, and the proclamation of the gospel through Word and Sacrament. The laity are no less called, however, to use their particular gifts in service to the whole.

It is important to have strong, equipped, committed laypeople in leadership roles within the congregation. Whether it be on the official board of the congregation, or teaching church school, or providing mentors for the youth program, this lay leadership not only provides the willing hands to do some of the work, they offer further stimulus to the visions and dreams that are shared with the pastor. This is one of the greatest gifts any congregation can provide for a pastor and, even if it does not ensure a long-term pastorate, goes a long way in creating congregational health and vitality. As a leader of any group knows, it is the people that surround them that help make all the difference in the environment of the working organization. By encouraging strong lay leadership the congregation supports not only the work within the body, but supports the pastor in the creative endeavors that help keep a congregation growing and alive.

5. Deal with Conflict Appropriately

The "Additional Reflections" part of the Alban study of long-term pastorates contains this statement: "Congregations which foster healthy long-tenured pastorates care for their own members as well as others outside the congregation, accept the clergy as human, allow room for failure, have a willingness to work with the clergy on common goals, use problem solving rather than blame in dealing with troublesome issues, and are open to new input, ideas, and members."[8] There is certainly a lot packed into that statement, which speaks to things a congregation can do to foster a long-term relationship with a pastor (some of those matters have already been covered in this chapter in slightly different language). However, the issue of using "problem solving rather than blame in dealing with troublesome issues" is one worth highlighting.

Any pastor who has served for longer than six months in ministry (a figure that may be shorter for some) knows that where two or three are gathered together, there is the very strong likelihood that at some time, perhaps when we least expect it, conflict will occur. Pastors who have been effective in long-term pastorates have developed a capacity to deal productively with such conflict. But the congregation also needs to learn how to do that. Often it is the pastor who models, teaches, and leads such efforts, but the congregation needs to learn how to do it too.

Many of us know congregations that have a reputation for being "difficult," if not impossible, to serve. They chew up and spit out clergy at an alarming rate. Either they never learned how to deal with conflict in healthy ways or they know no other way to operate and the pastor becomes the lightning rod for their displaced feelings. A congregation that wants to support a long-term pastorate needs to learn the skills necessary to allow conflict that will lead to productive ministry, not tear anyone down. If a pastor has to deal with brush fire after brush fire, to change the metaphor a moment, there will be little energy left to do the creative stuff that keeps her or him fresh for service. Learning how to fight is a good skill not only for marriages, but for pastor-parish relations as well. (For those who need help in this area, check out the resource list at the back of this book.)

6. Use the Pastor's Gifts Wisely

One of the best ways to frustrate anyone is to put him or her into a position where they cannot do that which they do well. Over the long haul (actually, over the short haul) that frustration will lead to some sort of change—either leaving or finding a way to use those gifts. A congregation that encourages the pastor's gifts and the use of those gifts within the faith community will diminish that frustration level considerably.

Obviously, in any job there are things that must be done that do not necessarily bring joy in the doing of them. If that is all we do, however, then either we are in the wrong field or in a mismatched work environment.

It is the gifts we have, when used and allowed to grow, that nourish our spirits and bring enthusiasm and joy into our ministries. For example, when the congregation I currently serve looked at my mobility papers from the judicatory they found out that one of the areas of ministry that I least enjoy is ministry with shut-ins. Don't get me wrong, I love the people. It just is not a part of ministry that energizes me. At one of the interviews, one of the search committee members saw that and asked if that meant that I would not be visiting their shut-ins. I responded by saying that although it is not one of the areas of ministry that I am either gifted at or find exciting, what my comment meant was that I would probably not accept a call where the congregation had 100 shut-ins and the expectation was that they be visited on a monthly basis. I did assure the man that I am faithful to my call and would visit their 12 shut-ins regularly, which I have done for the past 17 years. But I would be a lousy chaplain at a retirement home.

The matching of gifts with congregational needs and expectations starts in the interview and search process. A wise pastor and a wise congregation should be able to assess whether the gifts of the pastor match the presented needs of the congregation. However, an equally wise pastor and congregation, upon acceptance of the call, seek ways to encourage the use of the pastor's gifts both for her or his personal growth and the building-up of the body, which is how the Apostle Paul enjoins us to use all gifts from God.

Growing Up Together as Pastor and Congregation

Just as the seasons change and, year to year, each season brings the unexpected, so there are seasons in every person's life and every pastor's ministry. The only constant in life, besides death and taxes, is change. Nothing stays the same.

Pastor and author Lynne M. Baab has written about the seasons of ministry that are faced in serving in a single congregation for years.[9] Baab identifies (*a*) the *honeymoon* stage (which, as explained in chapter 3 of this book, may either not exist anymore or has become redefined as "trial by fire"); (*b*) the period of *disillusionment*; (*c*) the period of *trust building*, where the relationship between a pastor and a congregation becomes formed more firmly in reality and mutual respect; and (*d*) finally comes the *long haul of ministry*.

In and through these seasons, however, is the unpredictability caused by change. Pastors change over time. We discover new gifts and talents and seek to find ways to use them creatively. We mature in our understanding of others and self. We gain valuable experience that helps us to handle situations in better than "knee-jerk" reactions. We grow in our knowledge of scripture and learn, with each book read, more about ministry and its nuances.

The congregations we serve also do not stay stagnant. Change is a part of their lives as well. Church conflicts, major (or even minor) building programs, demographic changes to the community, the deaths of significant people in the parish, and economic conditions all contribute to the changes felt within a congregation.

Therefore, for a pastor and congregation to survive and actually thrive through the changes, both need to grow up together. There needs to be acknowledgement of the changes, mutual agreement on dealing with those changes, and support through the crises that such change can bring. Just like in a family, we learn to support, forgive, nurture, and stand with one another through the years.

Baab has also written a helpful book for pastors and congregations on how to embrace midlife change. Although addressed to that particular crisis, the suggestions given for how to cope can be effectively used for dealing with change during any stage of life. Baab interviewed pastors and rabbis and compiled their suggestions for how to negotiate a healthy midlife change. Among the unanimous suggestions were these:

- Do not neglect your own personal spiritual life
- Nurture friends outside of the congregation for balance and perspective
- Be rigorously honest with oneself before God
- Effectively use sabbatical and study leave[10]

Baab's article concludes with words that remind us of an important truth: "God is the author of nature's seasons, and God accompanies us through the seasons of our lives. We are not alone as we face the expected and the unexpected."[11] And that truth extends to all the phases and stages of growing up together as pastor and congregation as we travel over the long haul.

What Should We Do at the End of the Long Haul?

There is a one-word answer to the question just posed to which I would add a qualifier. What should we do at the end of the long haul? Leave. Leave well!

The best gift we can give our successor is to remember that our season in the sun as pastor of a congregation is over and that we, and they, need to move forward, perhaps in a new direction, but certainly with a new pastor in a different direction. Two books by Alban Institute consultants, Roy Oswald's *Running through the Thistles: Terminating a Ministerial Relationship with a Parish*, and Edward White's *Saying Goodbye: A Time for Growth for Congregations and Pastors*,[12] offer helpful ideas not only for how to deal with our own feelings of leaving, but also for how to have meaningful and healthy partings.

Certainly it is hard to say goodbye to a long-term relationship that has provided meaning, love, growth, and support for many years. But how we say goodbye can impact the congregation for many years to come, and clearly it impacts the next pastor.

In many judicatories, there is an intentional period of transition after a long-term pastorate. In some cases, a three- to four-year interim ministry is suggested so that the congregation can make the transition. And almost all judicatories have expectations of those who leave a parish as to what he or she can and cannot do back in that particular parish.

Alban consultant Terry Foland, in an article titled "Following a Beloved Pastor," speaks to the question, "How do I approach my new pastorate in the wake of a much-loved minister's leaving?" Foland offers the following five things to consider:

1. Help the congregation achieve closure.
2. Help the congregation understand its new relationship with the former pastor.
3. Make sure that the previous pastor has a similar understanding about the new relationship.
4. Be intentional about defining who you are and how you intend to engage in ministry with this congregation.
5. Be patient.[13]

As we examine this list for how a new pastor approaches such a situation, notice that the first three can also apply to the outgoing pastor and, I would contend, if done by the previous pastor, helps to make that transition to a new ministry easier. The most important of the five items to consider for our purposes here is number two—it is part of the responsibility of the outgoing pastor not only to understand that they are no longer the pastor of that parish, but to help the members of the parish to understand that as well.

In a word or two: Leave; leave well!

CHAPTER 9

Benediction and Sending
Blessings for the Journey

I told her I would walk the difficult path with her. I would be willing to share in the pain by listening to her anger, her fears, and her questions which have but few answers. I told her that I would not flinch, not preach, and not give glib and easy answers to the most difficult of life's questions. I would simply "be there" for the journey, and at the end, offer a benediction and blessing.

Sheila has pancreatic cancer. It is as aggressive as she was vibrant in life. She is not actually a member of the parish, but her brother and his family are, and they brought Sheila up from the South so that she could have the support and care of family. When hospice asked her about sending one of their chaplains to visit, she replied, "I have a pastor."

We had met years ago at the wedding of her youngest brother. Now, as she faces the most important journey of her life, she has invited me along to share in the discoveries along the way. It is a privilege that I hold in sacred trust; a privilege granted because of trust. I dare say, 10 years ago, her brother would not have known me well enough to ask if I would visit his sister. Now . . . a child of God will walk with another child of God on the way home.

It is a privilege known and enjoyed by very few in our society. We are invited to share in the most intimate, painful, and joyous times of people's lives. And it is our faithfulness during the long haul that makes those opportunities possible.

The Reverend Arthur F. Miessler, a Missouri Synod Lutheran pastor for 70 years, wrote about his ministry and passed that writing along to his children, the youngest of whom is a member of my parish, who shared this man's remarkable account of life in the ministry during a previous generation. Pastor Miessler wrote at the end of his memoirs as he reflected on ministry:

"During my ministry, I baptized 302, confirmed 254, performed 198 weddings, and 181 funerals. . . . It is the greatest privilege that any [person] can have."[1] As statistics go, those are not necessarily impressive numbers, until . . . until we stop to think about the lives touched, the moments shared, the intimacies known, and the hearts that were moved. This pastor appreciated the life to which God had called him.

The Destination Is Not as Important as the Journey

When we think about it, it is probably far easier to minister over the short haul than the long haul. In the short haul, we can recycle programs, repeat sermons, re-teach classes, draw from our knowledge bank, and, at least for those who are served, it seems new. And we can repeat this cycle in five-year periods throughout our ministry.

The long haul forces us to grow, to change, and to adapt over time. In the Alban research on long-term pastorates, the summary statement includes these words of encouragement for those in ministry: "In a long pastorate, clergy soon exhaust whatever wisdom or knowledge they brought to the scene and must continue to scramble to grow personally or end up repeating themselves and boring others. But those who do grow, who do monitor the other disadvantages of a long pastorate, will be likely to have a ministry that is very rewarding and fulfilling. They can experience a closeness and intimacy with people that comes only with time."[2]

It is the journey together that is ministry. The destination is not as important as the journey. It is on such a journey that we learn about ourselves. We discover gifts we didn't know we had. We find ever-creative ways to be authentic. We learn that the true essentials of ministry are not about theology, as important as that is, or about the number of meetings we need to attend. Ministry is about relationships: God and God's people; pastor and people; pastor and God. The long haul brings that clearly into focus and affords us the privilege of following God's call to be among God's people and to be about the proclamation of peace, reconciliation, and hope—a message this world so desperately needs to hear.

Faithfulness to Our Call

Max Lucado, in one of his books, compares the role of the Holy Spirit in our lives to a guy who wants to learn to dance. The metaphor is worth a look and a comment. This guy, you see, is rational, intelligent, and logical. He wants to learn to dance, so he does what he knows how to do—he goes to a bookstore and buys a book on "How to Dance." He takes it home and begins studying. He does everything it says with meticulous care. When the instructions say sway, he sways. When the instructions say lean, he leans. When the instructions say spin, he spins. He even cuts out paper footprints and arranges them on the family-room floor so he will know exactly where to step.

Finally, he thinks he's got it down pat. So, he calls his wife in and says, "Honey, watch!" With book in hand and reading aloud so she'll know he's done his homework, he follows the instructions, step by step. It says, "Take one step with your right foot." So, he takes one step with his right foot. Then it says, "Turn slowly to the left." He turns slowly to the left. He keeps it up, reading and then moving, reading and dancing, through the whole thing.

Then, he collapses exhausted on the sofa and says to his wife, "What do you think? I executed it perfectly!" To which she replies, "You executed it all right. You killed it!"

The confused husband says, "But I followed the rules. I laid out the pattern. I did everything the book said."

But his wife sighs, "You forgot the most important part. Where was the music?"

With that, she puts on a CD. "Try it now. Quit worrying about the steps and just follow the music." She holds out her hand, and he gets up and takes it. The music starts, and the next thing the guy knows he's dancing—without the book![3]

Lucado used this story, paraphrased rather freely here, to make a point about the Holy Spirit in our lives. But I want to expand the illustration a bit. There was something missing, to be sure—two things, in fact: the music and a partner.

Scripture certainly serves as the norm for faith and life within the church and there are countless other books out there that will help us with the various steps we need to master in order to do the dance of ministry. But without the music, without the calling from God who empowers such ministry, such steps are void of life. The music is supplied, as Lucado suggests, by God. But let us not forget that ministry is really partnership. It is pastor and people seeking to understand the will of God for them as a community of faith and finding creative ways to respond to that will.

It really all comes down to faithfulness. Maybe that should be the closing voice we hear on this topic of long-term pastorates. We seek to be faithful to the call we have received from God to serve where we feel God has called us to serve, using the gifts, training, and experience we have been given. Over the long haul that means we will have plenty of opportunities to grow, to expand, and to try new dance steps with this partner who is also changing, growing, and evolving.

In a world where stress and instability are deep realities in people's lives, we can be models of stability and support. We can be, as pastors, the anchors that help keep the people of God grounded in the reality of God's love and grace for their lives. Reverend Mark S. Hanson said as much in his first pastoral epistle since his call to be presiding bishop of the Evangelical Lutheran Church in America. Under the banner of "Staying Grounded," he wrote: "You who serve the church in these gathered communities are essential to the ministry [of the church], not only where you serve, but well beyond it. As you do the work to which God has called you, I encourage you to study God's Word, pray daily, worship regularly, and gather with others for support and encouragement. May God strengthen and uphold you."[4]

It is my sincere prayer that the ideas and thoughts of this book will be a source of insight for those either in long-term pastorates or who contemplate such a call. And, I hope my dialogue will contribute to further reflection on the issue of long-term pastorates. We who walk with the Sheilas of this world enjoy a marvelous privilege. And the further we walk, the longer we walk, the more we discover that the dance is one of blessing and life.

Lifting the Lid

Discovering More Questions Along the Way

The more I researched this issue of long-term pastorates and the more people to whom I talked about it, the more questions I discovered along the way. It was like lifting the lid on a giant box and seeing more inside than you could have imagined. So, this chapter will try to raise some of those questions in a way that invites those interested into further discussion and sharing.

No immediate answers to some of the questions probably exist and, in point of fact, providing answers is not the goal of this chapter. Instead, I intend to articulate some issues and offer some corresponding reflections and comments for consideration. Actually, two sets of questions follow: The first are questions with some thoughts attached and the second are questions that raise other questions. All are intended to stimulate further dialogue.

Questions with Reflections

* *If long-term pastorates are generally desirable, are pastorates actually getting longer?*

In other words, are judicatories making any progress in encouraging such pastorates? The research from two national church bodies seems to indicate that there have been no dramatic changes in clergy tenure over the past 10 years. Dr. Kenneth Inskeep, Director of Research for the Evangelical Lutheran Church in America, looked at all calls to congregations and determined what percent had been in place for 10, 20, and 30 years or more for the years 2001, 1995, and 1990.[1] The statistics are as follows:

	2001	1995	1990
10+ years =	17.9%	20.8%	19.8%
20+ years =	4.3%	5.3%	4.5%
30+ years =	0.7%	0.8%	0.8%

Statistics from the Presbyterian Church (USA) indicate a slight lengthening of calls, most dramatically in the mid-1990s, and a trend that has definitely continued during the last five years.

I was not able to check the statistics for other denominations, but it would be interesting to do so. Does the fact that more and more second-career people are entering the ministry affect long-term pastorates? Probably, but someone with better research skills than I would have to check that out.

- *How does the system of pastoral assignment affect long-term pastorates?*

Is there a difference in whether someone is assigned a call, as in the Methodist system, or goes through an open call process where choices can be made by both the pastor and the congregation? It used to be that persons in appointment systems would be moved around every four to six years, thus eliminating the possibility of a long-term pastorate. The theory behind that policy was that freshness and newness would be built into the system. However, this system also deprived pastors of the chance to develop trust so that relationships could move beyond the superficial level.

A call system, on the other hand, may work better to encourage long-term pastorates, but it is not without its negative aspects either. If the call system is complex, time consuming, and lengthy, it may "encourage pastors and congregations to maintain the status quo, i.e., to hold to a current call" (according to Reverend Jack Hoffman, former Assistant to the Bishop, Lower Susquehanna Synod, ELCA). The Right Reverend Robert Ihloff, Episcopal Bishop of Maryland, says something similar: "It is not productive for churches to have to go through this process every few years."

Therefore, making a good match in a call process seems to be the key. When asked the question, "What do you or your office do to support and encourage long-term pastorates?" Reverend Mary Zurell, Assistant to the

Bishop, Delaware-Maryland Synod, ELCA, says, "Facilitate good 'matches' between pastor and congregation."

- *Are there certain personalities that are better suited to long-term pastorates?*

The Alban research of 1983 indicated that this was an area worth further study. For instance, using the Myers-Briggs Personality Indicator, a person who is a "feeling"-oriented person is more vulnerable to the development of the "gap" (mentioned in chapter 5) than a "thinking"-oriented person.[2] On the other hand, "thinking"-oriented people tend to be more goal oriented and not only may be less aware of the feelings of people in any change effort, they may also tend to move on to new challenges once a particular goal is met.[3]

A proper fit of skills matched to the needs of a particular parish may be the most important issue. Reverend Guy Edmiston, a retired bishop in the ELCA who served for 14 years, believes that congregations, in encouraging long-term pastorates, should "insist on competency." The key, perhaps, is a combination of personality and skill-sets that meet the needs and expectations of the congregation.

- *Are there stages in a pastor's life and career that are more conducive to a long-term pastorate?*

At what stage in their career did today's long-term pastors enter into service in their congregation? There has always been this unspoken understanding that a pastor would remain in a long-term call if that call was her or his third or fourth call. It was always felt that one needed experience and maturing to serve in those calls. Is that still true today, especially in the light of second-career persons with life-experience entering the ministry later in life?

- *Are there significant events in a congregation's life that effect long-term pastorates?*

Any major change in area demographics may be one such event. Look at what has happened to many mainline inner-city congregations as a result of "white flight." Conversely, we have seen dramatic changes in congregations when there has been creative leadership that seeks to reach out to the community around it and develop relationships and service. In changing neighborhoods, one of the places of stability and support can be the local parish, and if the pastor chooses to stay during such times of change and become that stability, the congregation has the opportunity to do dynamic and creative, albeit changing, ministry.

Another event in a congregation's life that might affect a pastorate's length would be a major building program. I heard one time that something like 80 percent of pastors who lead a congregation through such programs leave within two years of completing the project.

- *Is the size of a congregation an issue for further study?*

Bishop Don McCoid of the Southwestern Pennsylvania Synod of the ELCA perhaps gives voice to an unspoken assumption when he writes: "We try to offer pastors opportunities to serve in congregations where they can have longer-term ministries, especially if the congregation is a larger-membership parish." Is this true in other denominations?

It is probably the case that more large congregations than small ones have long-term pastorates because they have more resources to keep up with the financial expectations of a pastor over a long haul. But if long-term pastorates are considered healthy for congregations, how can such pastorates be encouraged and supported for congregations of all sizes?

- *Relatedly, is the setting of a congregation a factor?*

Different dynamics and expectations clearly differentiate congregations that are in urban, suburban, town-and-country, and rural settings. Is there one setting that seems to encourage long-term pastorates more than the other pastoral settings? What are the dynamics that make that happen? Are there congregations that expect long-term pastorates and who have encouraged a number of them within their own history?

Further Issues to Ponder:
Questions That Raise More Questions

The last four questions above could easily fall into the category of the questions that are about to be raised because they tend to engender many more questions than answers at this point. Here are a few more to consider:

- *Are there certain crises that can affect long-term pastorates?*

Loss of trust due to clergy misconduct comes to mind, but there may be others.

- *Is congregational membership turnover an issue?*

When there is rapid turnover in a congregation's membership, there is also a turnover in leadership. This can lead to freshness and newness, but can also cause a pastor to tire of the need to always bring new people "on board."

- *As a congregation (and a pastor) changes over time is there a change in leadership style? Is it a factor to consider?*

What happens when the pastor's skills do not match the change that has taken place? Can a long-term pastor learn to adjust in style to meet those changes? Conversely, if the pastor goes through any significant change over time, like loss of a spouse or health issues, can the congregation learn to adjust to the changes those situations can cause? Can lay leadership begin to take on new roles if a pastor's energies begin to fade?

- *Are there situations that may cause a long-term pastorate "by default?"*

Being geographically restricted due to a spouse's occupation or career would be one. The pastor being a certain age might be another (there is age-bias in congregations even today). How about fiscal considerations? Maybe a pastor is so well paid that she or he cannot afford to move. If the only reasons a pastor stays in a given situation are external ones, would that count as being a long-term pastorate "by default?"

- *What impact does the pastor's family have on a long-term pastorate?*

The career of a spouse has already been mentioned, but what about the ages of children? There has always been folk wisdom that says the best time to move would be before children start middle school or after they finish high school. Does that wisdom still apply? Are there other factors, like the age of a pastor's own parents and their future needs, to consider when thinking about moving?

Now What?

At the end of paragraphs and paragraphs of questions one might be tempted to ask yet one more: So what? What do all the questions mean? What do they tell us?

They tell us, first of all, that there is a lot we simply do not know. Researchers will have to shed light on some of the issues. For the rest, we need to share our stories with one another so that the accumulated experiences we bring to the discussion table can continue to inform, enlighten, and teach us.

But perhaps there is a more obvious insight that comes after the lid of this topic has been lifted a bit. Ministry is a dynamic relationship between a pastor and a congregation that is ever-changing and multifaceted. It is the reason why no two days in the life of a pastor are ever the same. It is the reason why no two years in the life of a congregation are ever the same. And it is that dynamic which challenges those of us who are called into service to ask these sorts of questions that can lead to further growth, awareness, and health.

There are more questions that surround the issue of long-term pastorates. I hope that this appendix will actually raise even more of them for the thoughtful and reflective pastors of the church.

Wisdom Borne of Experience
Hearing from the Survivors

In the course of putting this book together I had the opportunity to talk to a number of pastors and consultants from a variety of denominations. Since each one obviously had something important to contribute, I have added this appendix on "wisdom borne of experience," to allow their voices to be heard.

I sent "A Brief Survey on Long-Term Pastorates" to 40 pastors (25 men and 15 women), representing 15 different denominations, inviting them to share their experiences and wisdom. This, obviously, is not a large survey as surveys go, but it is representational. The persons invited had met at least one of the following criteria: (1) are currently serving in a long-term pastorate; (2) attended the Alban Institute seminar on "New Visions for the Long Pastorate"; and/or (3) were chosen by me because I felt they had something to offer.

Fifteen pastors returned the survey (16 men and 4 women), representing nine denominations. For easy reference, their names, churches served, cities, and denominations are listed at the end of this chapter. Therefore, as we allow them voice through this chapter, only the name will be referenced. All of them have given permission to use their comments and insights. Because it seems important to hear their wisdom, I will try to keep editorial comments to a minimum, only trying to summarize collective thoughts where appropriate to do so.

The survey consisted of six questions, which shall be taken in turn. As I have stated previously, I am not a researcher by trade. Therefore, what is being shared here is not a scientific approach to long-term pastorates, but rather a pastoral one. We will allow those who serve to speak here.

One final background note is in order. The years served in their current call of the 15 pastors who completed the survey ranges from six to 23 years, with the average somewhere between 12 and 15. (One pastor who had attended the Alban seminar did complete part of the form but confessed that after the seminar he "found out that he did not share similar goals with the church" and left that call [George Saunders].) All of the pastors surveyed represent a wealth of accumulated experience and wisdom that is worth sharing.

Brief Survey on Long-Term Pastorates

1. *When did you feel that you had "arrived" in your current call? How long did it take you to get established?*
The answers to these two questions ranged from one year to 10 years, with the consensus average between five and seven years. Some pastors did make a distinction between "arriving" and "getting established." Bill Inglish wrote that arrival took "probably four years. I had been here seven years before any major changes." Likewise, Bruce Cochran said, "At the six-year mark, I felt established. . . . However, I have found that it is a continual process." Lynn Groe, from a perspective of 16 years serving his current congregation, made the distinction this way: "[The] first 1 to 3 years were getting-acquainted time, settling in to the new pastorate. . . . From 5 to 10 years—these seemed to be very effective years, they went by very fast."

In answering these two questions, some pastors offered benchmarks that helped them to realize when they had arrived. Those benchmarks included: leadership transitions ("[I] knew I had made it when new people stepped up to assume leadership" [Barbara Kershner Daniel]); conflict resolution ("I had feelings of 'arrival' when, in a conflict situation, the council supported me and not the 'troublemaker'" [Beth R. Lupolt]; "I felt I had 'arrived' after guiding the congregation through healing following 10 years of major conflict" [Steven Grosvenor]); and pastoral care opportunities ("The church experienced some painful losses of members during that period [the first 18 months of my pastorate] due to death or transfer, and my ability to 'be with them' through those losses seemed to cement my relationship with this church" [Dan Holloway]).

2. *What have been your joys and blessings?*
By far the number one answer to this question centered on pastoral relationships with people, especially officiating at important stages in

parishioner's lives. It is a common litany filled with the ultimate joys of parish ministry. Listen:

- "[My joys and blessings include] seeing children I held as babies choose to be baptized and own the faith as young adults; officiating the marriages of those whom I baptized as young adults." (Linford King)
- "My joys and blessings center on the church family—my long years here have rooted me in people's lives." (Patricia Evans)
- "[My joy has been] to see the congregation develop a greater level of intimacy." (Dave Bushnell)

A second area of joy and blessing named by many came from working alongside others, both lay and clergy, in ministry.

- "I have been blessed by lots of talented lay people who are willing to give of themselves to me both personally and professionally, and in leadership in the church." (William R. Shiflet, Jr.)
- "Basically, I am surrounded by 'good' people." (Steven H. Albers)
- "[A joy has been] the successful growth of our staff." (Holloway)

A third area that brought joy and blessings to some pastors could fall under the general heading of pastoral leadership and its effect on both the congregation and the surrounding community. A strongly identified joy has been:

- "'Recreating' an old but wonderful congregation—seeing the fruits of my ministry and leadership." (John Sabatelli)
- "Reorganizing of the church board to improve involvement of people." (Grosvenor)
- "Gaining respect as a community leader." (Bruce Cochran)

These pastors obviously view ministry as a great privilege and most of their joys and blessings come from relationships of trust that not only allow them to touch people's lives at significant times and in significant ways, but also allow them the opportunity to use that trust to lead a congregation forward in ministry. One pastor even counted two building programs as among his joys. However, he was quick to add, "I count those as a joy (now that we are finished!)" [Holloway]. Those among us who have been there and done that are probably sure of that!

3.   *What has been the key for you in making your ministry effective?*
The answers to this question revealed the most diversity, and yet the most
comprehensive, of answers. The pastors surveyed clearly knew and were
able to articulate what the keys have been for them. Without doing injustice
to the individual answers, the keys for effective ministry could be summarized
around five specific points:

A.   *Love the people.* This was the number one answer, well said in the
     following statements:

     •   "I think the key to a successful long-term pastorate is to love your
         people through thick and thin, through the good times and the bad.
         I had a young pastor ask me when they had found out that I have
         been in my current congregation for over 12 years, 'How do you
         keep the people loving you that long?' I replied, 'You love them
         back!'" (Groe)
     •   "It probably sounds trite, but . . . loving the people! Congregations
         know when you love them, and if a pastor is willing to weather the
         storms and hang in there, the 'staying power' goes far toward
         effective ministry." (Lupolt)
     •   "Personal relationships. People need to know that I care for and
         with them." (Albers)
     •   "Love the people." (Cochran)

B.   *Patience.* The number two answer, and somewhat of a surprise, comes
     with the subtitle of "taking the long view" of things. Here is a sampling
     of the responses:

     •   "Take it easy! Meaning—don't push so hard." (Evans)
     •   "Patience in 'outliving' the opposition." (Sabatelli)
     •   "I tend not to get overly excited in times of stress, at least externally."
         (Holloway)
     •   "Being a nonanxious presence." (King)
     •   "Patience." (Cochran)

C.   *Developing the support of leadership.* Since we probably work with
     the leadership of the church the hardest, the longest, and the most
     intensively, this answer does not come as any great surprise. In pastoral

ministry, however, I think this is an area that is taken either too lightly or too much for granted.

- "Garnering the support of leadership." (Inglish)
- "My willingness to ask people to participate and be the personnel director in some respects." (Shiflet)
- "Foster relationships with leadership; [I] once was told that the most important committee is 'nominating'—[you] need to have people with whom you can do ministry, who share vision." (Albers)

D. *Sabbaticals*. I could add my own comments here on the importance of planned time away, but that was covered in an earlier chapter. So, we will let others add their support:

- "Sabbaticals have been ESSENTIAL to my ability to stay in the same congregational setting. . . . Besides [being] a restful time for me, I have always returned from sabbaticals with new ideas and plans." (Bushnell)
- One pastor simply wrote, in answer to what has been the key, "Sabbaticals!" (Kershner Daniel)

E. *Skills and values for the journey together.* These can be further delineated into two types: *task skills* (like preaching) and *personal values* (like honesty). Most of the pastors who answered the survey felt that some form of their skills were needed and appreciated by the congregation and that these were an important key to their effectiveness over the long haul.

- Albers combined the two in his answer: "Honesty. What they see is what they get. . . . Good preaching and preparing worship— that's subjective, of course, but [I] work hard at that."
- "The key to making my ministry effective has been, number one, 'my blunt, straightforward, intentional approach that pays attention to detail.'" (Shiflet)
- "Hard work, long hours, dedication, and some God-given talents for preaching, teaching, and administration." (Sabatelli)

As I commented at the outset of this question, the answers were very comprehensive and thoughtful. It is a tribute to the ministry of these pastors that they are both aware of what makes them effective and, like good stewards, are thankful for the gifts God has given them and are willing to work hard to develop those gifts for ministry.

4. *What challenges and conflicts have you experienced?*
This question also elicited a fair range of responses, but again some recurrent themes appeared on the surveys. By and large, however, the pastors surveyed did not use this opportunity to "vent" their frustrations, angers, or disappointments, but rather they simply shared what they had experienced with a marked degree of thought and reflection. Here are the themes that seemed to be repeated with some slight variations because of individual expression:

A. *Growth and change.* The conflicts mentioned seemed to center around the issue of "Whose church is it anyway?" and "What's happening to my church?" Let's give the voice over to the pastors:

- "The conflict between the 'good old boys' (old guard) in the congregation and the new blood. The frustration with this one is that this is often the main problem but is only covered up by surface issues." (Cochran)
- "Most of our challenges have been around issues of growth. Some, though not many, long-time members have found the loss of familiarity to be especially painful, and have moved to other churches or fallen into inactivity." (Holloway)
- "Resistance to new people. Feelings of 'entitlement' by long-time members." (Barbara Blaisdell)
- "A transition in leadership. . . . Charter members have had to relinquish control." (King)
- "The greatest challenge of our congregation has been growth. I don't mean that we are striving to grow in leaps and bounds, but recently we have looked very long and hard at congregational size theory. . . . Moving up to a more program-centered congregation has helped us understand the conflicts (or patterns of avoiding conflicts) in the congregation's life." (Bushnell)
- "It was a challenge for many to accept a woman as senior pastor. It was a double challenge to accept a liberal woman as pastor." (Evans)

B. *Staffing issues.* No doubt this identified cause of conflict and challenge only applies to congregations who have staffs. However, it is a major issue for those who live and work with such. At an Alban seminar for senior pastors, this is identified as the number one concern, problem, and challenge. If we polled associate pastors, my hunch would be that they would identify the same issue. Here are the pastors who spoke about this in their words:

- "Personnel. We're not always on the same wavelength." (Albers)
- "Colleagues and staff conflicts. Having to fire a staff member." (Shiflet)
- "There have been the biggest challenges with the calling and retaining of staff." (Kershner Daniel)
- "The first staffperson lasted four years, he was a seminary graduate ... but he left the congregation poorly, continued to maintain contact with his supporters, and complained often about me." (Groe)

For persons called into staff ministry, there are significant challenges to be dealt with. But when those relationships work, ministry increases exponentially.

C. *Building programs.* Anyone who has ever been through a building program in the church knows the frustrations of this time-consuming ministry. Everything seems to take twice as long as anticipated and cost twice the estimates. Having lived through two major building programs I can honestly say I am glad we did what we had to do and I pray to God everyday that we do not do another one in my lifetime! Enough from me. Here are some of the pastors who have lived to voice their challenges in this area:

- "Our building campaign. Bids came in at twice our estimate. We were only able to do half of what we'd proposed. Burnout and bitterness of leadership through that process. It's taken us three years to recover and we're not there yet." (Inglish)
- "Building program! It brings out the worst in people. The challenge is to also allow it to build cohesiveness in creative differing." (Lupolt)

(Perhaps my next book will be *How to Negotiate the Rapid Waters of a Building Program*, or, *What I Would Do with My Time If We Didn't Build!*)

D. *History of the congregation.* This may be a subset of the first challenge regarding growth and change, but it seemed significant enough in its own right to warrant a separate heading. My hunch is that this is an issue that many of us have moved past and, maybe, have forgotten (maybe even forgiven!). It is a significant issue if the history of the congregation includes a conflict that still has the power to hurt and harm. Listen:

   • "Ten years of conflict had diminished my leaders and demoralized the people. Talk of relocation had postponed appropriate maintenance on their building. They were in some ways suspicious of pastors and fragmented as a congregation. They had also isolated themselves from the community." (Grosvenor)

There is no doubt that serving in ministry is one of the most challenging of callings in this world. What these pastors spoke of are real issues they have faced as they have tried to be true to themselves and their callings. The pastors were honest, forthright, candid, and, I suspect, a bit bruised from the conflicts. It is the hard part of ministry to have to deal with some of these issues and is why the title of this chapter has the word survivors in it.

5. *How have you balanced the issues of personal freedom and shared leadership in your congregational setting?*

There are three obvious, or perhaps not-so-obvious, factors that affected the answers to this question. The first was the particular *denomination* of the pastor. There is a wide range of practices and polities in the church. Some churches, for instance, automatically give the pastor a large dose of freedom to make decisions, determine policies, and set the course for the ministry; others restrict such freedoms. A rector of an Episcopal church has much more authority than the senior pastor of a Lutheran congregation. Rector Bill Shiflet, Jr., spoke of his role: "I have made it clear in my contract, my overall responsibility and authority in relation to the program within the church and the hiring, supervision, and accountability of staff in that regard."

He then adds: "I have shared that authority on most occasions and work collaboratively with parish leaders in making decisions."

The second factor affecting the answers to the question was the *history of the congregation and its pastors*. In other words, what has been the traditional role of the pastor in that setting of ministry? John Sabatelli, who serves a center-city church with a unique and rich history, writes: "[This church's tradition is] of following its pastor and giving him a great deal of authority and respect."

The third factor to consider has to do with the personality, style, and gifts of the pastor. How the pastor understands his or her pastoral role, how that pastor uses the gifts of God in leadership, and what style of leadership is most natural to her or him all affect the way a pastor would answer this particular question. Lynn Groe spoke of this when he wrote in answer to the question, "I have a pretty laid-back style and try to go with the flow of activities. . . . I have found that I have a great deal of personal freedom as a pastor to do the things that I do best."

By far the consensus of those surveyed talked about shared leadership being a goal in their ministries. Said another way, the goal of pastoral leadership is shared leadership. This consensus crossed denominational lines, and even personality and style differences. Here is a sampling of the answers:

- "I have had a great deal of freedom in my own leadership role of the congregation. . . . In fact, the church has depended too much on its pastoral leadership. Sharing leadership is gradually happening as more and more people are helping us establish priorities for the future." (Bushnell)
- "Ironically, I have discovered that shared leadership actually contributes to and promotes more personal pastoral freedom. I make very few unilateral decisions, but I enjoy a large amount of latitude to do so. My parishioners rarely question my use of 'pastoral power,' probably because I invite them at every turn to do so." (Lupolt)

There is one more unique feature of the answers received that should be mentioned. Under the banner of "shared leadership," there came the phrase over and over again, "This is not 'my' church." It seems that even as pastors seek to use their pastoral gifts for leadership within a congregation, there is an underlying awareness of an important fact that they always keep in mind—this is not "my" church. It might be best just to listen to that mantra from the perspective of three pastors:

- "The more trust has grown, the more freedom I have to be creative and push for change, but the harder it is to delegate. . . . I have to 'let go' and remember that this church is not 'my' church and everything does not have to be according to my standards." (Evans)
- "This is not 'my' church. . . . Therefore, I 'listen' and wait and refuse to push my agenda. As I have gained credibility and trust, my ideas are more likely to be embraced." (King)
- "One thing that helps put this in perspective [the issue of personal freedom and shared leadership] is to watch myself so I don't begin to think and act as if this is 'my' church." (Cochran)

6. *What words of wisdom would you share with those about to begin their journey toward a long-term pastorate?*

There is not enough space for the purposes of this chapter to listen to all that was shared by way of "words of wisdom." The voices, however, were strong, confident, and filled with encouragement for those thinking about or planning to be involved in a long-term pastorate.

Theological viewpoints and pieties surfaced for some of the participants. A few felt that pastors really do not "decide" about such matters. Steven Albers wrote: "[I'm] not sure that anyone can prepare for a long-term pastorate; the Holy Spirit has something to do with that." This view was echoed by Lynn Groe: "I am not sure that you can simply 'decide' to stay for a long time in one place. The call of the Holy Spirit has governed me throughout these past 17 years."

In answering the question, many spoke of the values and benefits to the congregation of long term pastorates:

- "I think it's the only way to establish long-term change in a congregation. In these difficult days for the church, those whose pastors stick around will be the few who can really make a difference." (Inglish)
- "It takes years to truly see and understand a congregation's vision. . . . If you have what it takes to help a congregation fulfill its vision—stay." (Evans)
- "It's worth it! It takes a long time for change to happen." (Kershner Daniel)

Finally, some pastors simply gave advice that is worth passing on to those about to begin their journeys. For those with ears to hear and eyes set toward the long view:

- "Have a strong philosophy of ministry, a clear understanding of your ordination, and a clear definition of pastoral ministry." (Grosvenor)
- "Understand the importance and value of the passing of time. . . . Commit to the long view and measure effectiveness at that level." (Cochran)
- "Really work hard to continue to be excited about the ministry that you have together. Expect cycles. Plan sabbaticals. Honor the past. Be pulled toward the future." (Bushnell)

A Final Word—and Appreciation

Although my survey sample was small, it nevertheless contained wisdom and insights that only those who serve, survive, and, ultimately, thrive, can offer. I am grateful for the participation of those who took the time to reflect on ministry for the long haul. Their words needed little exegesis and even less interpretation for they spoke clearly and plainly about the issues before all of us.

To acknowledge their participation and by way of showing appreciation for their words, here is the listing of those who completed the surveys, complete with their names, congregation served, location, and denomination (where all this data is known). May your words bring insight, courage, hope, and strength for those about to begin this wonderful journey.

Survey Participants

Steven H. Albers: Glendale Lutheran Church, Glendale, Missouri (Lutheran Church—Missouri Synod)

Barbara S. Blaisdell: First Christian Church, Clayton, California (Christian Church [Disciples of Christ])

Dave Bushnell: Hamilton Park United Church of Christ, Lancaster, Pennsylvania (United Church of Christ)

Bruce Cochran: First Baptist Church, Seymore, Indiana (American Baptist)

Barbara Kershner Daniel: St. Paul's United Church of Christ, Fleetwood, Pennsylvania (United Church of Christ)

Patricia Evans: First Christian Church, Selma, California (Christian Church [Disciples of Christ])

Lynn G. Groe: St. John's Lutheran Church, Waukon, Iowa (Evangelical Lutheran Church in America)

Steven R. Grosvenor: Church of the Nazarene, New Cumberland, Pennsylvania (Church of the Nazarene)

Dan Holloway: Unity Presbyterian, Ft. Mill, South Carolina (Presbyterian Church—USA)

Bill Inglish: First Christian Church, Stillwater, Oklahoma (Christian Church [Disciples of Christ])

Linford King: Neffsville Mennonite Church, Lancaster, Pennsylvania (Mennonite)

Beth R. Lupolt: St. Luke Lutheran Church, Chambersburg, Pennsylvania (Evangelical Lutheran Church in America)

John Sabatelli: Christ Lutheran Church, Baltimore, Maryland (Evangelical Lutheran Church in America)

George Saunders: American Baptist (currently leading an ecumenical agency)

William R. Shiflet, Jr.: St. John's Episcopal Church, Ellicott City, Maryland (Episcopal)

Chapter 2

1. William H. Willimon, *Calling and Character* (Nashville: Abingdon Press, 2000), 2.

2. Roy M. Oswald, Gail D. Hinand, William Chris Hobgood, and Barton M. Lloyd, *New Visions for the Long Pastorate* (Washington, D.C.: The Alban Institute, 1983), 29-30.

Chapter 3

1. Andrew Greeley, "Are Lay Catholics Getting Their Money's Worth?" *Context* (Chicago: Claretian Publications, 2001), 3.

2. Richard C. Weber, "The Group: A Cycle from Birth to Death," in *Reading Book for Human Relations Training* (Arlington, Va.: National Training Laboratories, 1982), 68-71.

Chapter 4

1. Ronald A. Heifetz, *Leadership without Easy Answers* (Cambridge, Mass.: Belknap Press, 1994), 2.

2. Gil Rendle, "The Leadership We Need" *Congregations* 27, no. 5 (Sept./Oct. 2001): 4.

3. L. Gregory Jones and Susan Pendleton Jones, "Pivotal Leadership," *Christian Century* (Sept. 12-19, 2001), 24.

4. Heifetz, *Leadership without Easy Answers*, 15.

5. Gil Rendle, "But What Should We Do About That?" *Congregations* 26, no. 3 (May/June 2000): 21.

6. Anthony B. Robinson, "Leadership That Matters," *Christian Century* (December 15, 1999), 1228.

Chapter 5

1. Roy M. Oswald, Gail D. Hinand, William Chris Hobgood, and Barton M. Lloyd, *New Visions for the Long Pastorate* (Washington, D.C.: The Alban Institute, 1983), 42-71.

2. The Samaritan Institute, The Samaritan Health and Living Center, Inc., Elkhart, Indiana.

3. Shannon L. Pearson, "Why Pastors Leave the Ministry," *Church Executive* 1, no. 1 (January 2002): 22.

4. Ibid., 21.

5. William H. Willimon, *Clergy and Laity Burnout* (Nashville: Abingdon Press, 1989), 25.

6. Adapted from Roy M. Oswald, *Clergy Self-Care: Finding a Balance for Effective Ministry* (Bethesda, Md.: The Alban Institute, 1991), 68.

7. Roy M. Oswald, *Why You Should Give Your Pastor a Sabbatical* (Bethesda, Md.: The Alban Institute, 2001).

8. Oswald et. al., *New Visions for the Long Pastorate*, 42-47.

9. Ibid., 68.

Chapter 7

1. Interlink Consultants, Ltd., *How to Supervise Church Staff and Volunteers* (Overland Park, Kans: Interlink Seminars, 1988), 1.

2. John C. Maxwell, *The 21 Irrefutable Laws of Leadership* (Nashville: Thomas Nelson Publishers, 1998), 109-119.

3. Ibid., 113.

4. Interlink Consultants, *How to Supervise Church Staff*, 12.

5. R. Paul Stevens and Phil Collins, *The Equipping Pastor: A Systems Approach to Congregational Leadership* (Bethesda, Md..: The Alban Institute, 1993), xii.

6. Norman Shawchuck, *How to Be a More Effective Church Leader* (Glendale Heights, Ill.: Organizational Resources Press, Spiritual Growth Resources, 1981), 6.

7. Stevens and Collins, *The Equipping Pastor*, 19-37.

8. Robert B. Blake and Jane S. Mouton, *The Managerial Grid*, III (Houston: Gulf Publishing Co., 1985), 12.

9. Stevens and Collins, *The Equipping Pastor*, 58.

10. Ken Blanchard, Patricia Zigarmi, and Drea Zigarmi, *Leadership and the One Minute Manager: Increasing Effectiveness through Situational Leadership* (New York: William Morrow, 1985).

11. Ibid., 33.

12. Ibid., 30.

Chapter 8

1. Lyle E. Schaller, *The Multiple Staff and the Large Church* (Nashville: Abingdon Press, 1980), 57.

2. Roy M. Oswald, Gail D. Hinand, William Chris Hobgood, and Barton M. Lloyd, *New Visions for the Long Pastorate* (Washington, D.C.: The Alban Institute, 1983), 32.

3. Ibid. 40.

4. Roy M. Oswald, *Why You Should Develop a Pastor-Parish Relations Committee* (Bethesda, Md. The Alban Institute, 2001).

5. Oswald et al., *New Visions for the Long Pastorate*, 39.

6. Ibid.

7. Ibid., 40.

8. Ibid., 41.

9. Lynne M. Baab, "Unpredictable Seasons," *Congregations* 28, no. 1 (Jan/Feb. 2002): 19.

10. Lynne M. Baab, *Embracing Midlife: Congregations as Support Systems* (Bethesda, Md.: The Alban Institute, 1999), 139-146.

11. Baab, "Unpredictable Seasons," 21.

12. Roy M. Oswald, *Running through the Thistles: Terminating a Ministerial Relationship with a Parish* (Washington, D.C.: The Alban Institute, 1978); Edward White, *Saying Goodbye: A Time for Growth for Congregations and Pastors* (Washington, D.C.: The Alban Institute, 1990).

13. Terry Foland, "Following a Beloved Pastor," *Congregations* 28, no. 1 (Jan/Feb. 2002): 36.

Chapter 9

1. Personal Memoirs of the Rev. Arthur F. Miessler (1889-1984).

2. Roy M. Oswald, Gail D. Hinand, William Chris Hobgood, and Barton M. Lloyd, *New Visions for the Long Pastorate* (Washington, D.C.: The Alban Institute, 1983), 87-88.

3. Rubel Shelly, "Great Themes of the Bible: Spirits Indwelling," *Faith Matters*, www.faithmatters.faithsite.com.

4. Mark S. Hanson, Presiding Bishop's Easter 2002 Letter (Chicago, Illinois), 2.

Appendix 1

1. I need to acknowledge that there are more ELCA sources quoted or acknowledged in this book than any other denomination. Because I am not a researcher by profession, I did not have easy access to other denominational data. I am sure that statistics from other sources that might support or contradict these findings are available from other denominational sources.

2. Roy M. Oswald, Gail D. Hinand, William Chris Hobgood, and Barton M. Lloyd, *New Visions for the Long Pastorate* (Washington, D.C.: The Alban Institute, 1983), 52.

3. Ibid., 54.

Help for the Long Haul

There are many facets and sides to parish ministry. Obviously, seminary training concentrates on the academic side of the calling, but there is much, much more to be learned. We need to understand human dynamics and interpersonal relationships, leadership styles, management skills, time-management techniques, and much more. The following resources are those that are relevant to the issues discussed in this book. Many of them deal with the "how-to" areas of long-term pastorates—how to, for instance, set up a Pastor-Parish Relations Committee, or how to develop a sabbatical plan. Many of these resources were referenced within the book, but there was not enough time or room to go into much detail. I hope that this resource list will help those who wish to delve more deeply into any of the specific areas relevant to long-term pastorates. Annotations are adapted from the Congregational Resource Guide Web site (www.congregationalresources.org), where further resources may be located. Happy reading!

Clergy Self-Care

Books

Berglas, Steven. *Reclaiming the Fire: How Successful People Overcome Burnout.*
New York: Random House, 2001.
Steven Berglas has written a psychological treatise on success and burnout that can help church people who give and receive vocational ministry. Focusing on persons who have demonstrated both success and disorientation in their work, Berglas says that to reclaim passion, we must recover ambition in new and healthy ways. This book could serve as a text for a leadership retreat or adult education course—particularly in a congregation where parishioners are experiencing career burnout.

Hands, Donald R., and Wayne L. Fehr. *Spiritual Wholeness for Clergy: A New Psychology of Intimacy with God, Self, and Others*. Bethesda, Md.: The Alban Institute, 1993.
Donald Hands and Wayne Fehr draw from over 10,000 hours of clinical therapy and spiritual direction with clergy. They describe the various disorders and pathologies that clergy suffer, summarize the phases of healing, and spell out a healthy spirituality in relationship with self, others, and God.

Melander, Rochelle, and Harold Eppley. *The Spiritual Leader's Guide to Self-Care*. Bethesda, Md.: The Alban Institute, 2002.
Melander and Eppley's book is an ideal companion for clergy, lay leaders, and others who would like guidance about how to make changes in their personal lives and ministries but do not want to read a text-heavy book about self-care. Readers may work through one of the 52 sections each week or adopt a more leisurely pace. The guide includes journal-writing suggestions, personal reflection questions and activities, guidance for sharing the discovery process with another person, an activity for the coming week, and suggested further resources.

Oswald, Roy M. *Clergy Self-Care: Finding a Balance for Effective Ministry*. Bethesda, Md.: The Alban Institute, 1991.
Roy Oswald's classic book on clergy self-care provides a number of strategies for dealing with the stresses of clergy life. By offering effective self-evaluation tools, Oswald convinces clergy that they often suffer stress and face the prospect of burnout. Churches need to recognize that they will benefit from knowing more about the elements of clergy stress. Oswald's strategies include holistic approaches to body and soul, spiritual direction, self-assertiveness, and letting go.

Shawchuck, Norman, and Roger Heuser. *Leading the Congregation: Caring for Yourself while Serving the People*. Nashville: Abingdon Press, 1993.
Leading the Congregation provides a survey course on the roles, functions, and pitfalls of congregational leadership. The authors cite the conditions that constrain a pastor's leadership efforts, discuss the pastoral inner journey, and attend to the interplay between pastoral authority and the authority of the congregation. While this is an excellent starter for new clergy, seasoned pastors also should take this book off the shelf at the inception of any new pastorate.

Vineyard, Sue. *How to Take Care of You . . . So You Can Take Care of Others*. Downers Grove, Ill.: Heritage Arts Publishing, 1989.
The author believes that human service workers and volunteers in a

variety of venues are at high risk of physical, emotional, mental, and spiritual depletion. Drawing deeply on her personal story of stress-related illness and her experience serving as a national trainer and consultant, Vineyard explores change, grief, stress, dimensions of depletion and wellness, and methods of gaining balance. The book will interest people who seek greater self-care and leaders who wish to build healthier and more respectful systems for volunteers and caregivers.

Wimberly, Edward P. *Recalling Our Own Stories: Spiritual Renewal for Religious Caregivers*. San Francisco: Jossey-Bass, 1997.
Pastor and seminary professor Edward Wimberly believes that by "reauthoring" the stories or "mythology" (unresolved personal problems or uncompleted developmental tasks) from their personal, familial, and ministerial lives, ministers can become more effective. Religious caregivers, who are often vulnerable emotionally, will have more to offer as they experience growth and healing. Anyone involved in religious caregiving will find this resource helpful. It could be used for personal reflection, in classes, or on leadership retreats.

Video

Oswald, Roy. *Why You Should Develop a Pastor-Parish Relations Committee*. Bethesda, Md.: The Alban Institute, 2001.
Alban consultant Roy Oswald puts forth a new vision for the role of the pastor-parish relations (or "mutual ministry") committee, suggesting that the group's sole task is to monitor the quality of the relationship between the pastor and the congregation. Rather than fielding complaints, conducting evaluations, or setting salary, committee members should work to understand the pastor's perspective, hopes, and needs, and to convey to the pastor their understanding of the congregation's life. A leader guide outlines use of the video to work with a board and members.

Sabbaticals

Books

Bullock, Richard A., and Richard J. Bruesehoff. *Clergy Renewal: The Alban Guide to Sabbatical Planning*. Bethesda, Md.: The Alban Institute, 2000.
Pastoral sabbaticals can help keep ministry vital and growing for the

long term. The authors provide a guide for planning a sabbatical and discuss the benefits for both the pastor and the congregation. The book also includes practical advice on sabbatical policies, rituals for sending and welcoming back the pastor, funding possibilities, and places to go while on sabbatical.

Sevier, Melissa Bane. *Journeying toward Renewal: A Spiritual Companion for Pastoral Sabbaticals*. Bethesda, Md.; The Alban Institute, 2002.
Melissa Bane Sevier used her own pastoral sabbatical to create this spiritually nourishing resource that helps to shepherd pastors through the unknowns of renewal leave. Drawing on the author's own journal entries, *Journeying toward Renewal* is a deeply personal guide that demonstrates powerful insight into the joys and stresses of pastoral ministry. Along with engaging reflections on the experience of preparing for and being on sabbatical, the book includes thought-provoking exercises, activities, ideas, and resources to help readers get the most out of renewal leave.

Organization

National Clergy Renewal Program
This program of Lilly Endowment Inc. provides financial support for rest and renewal to pastors of Christian congregations. Applications are made by congregations, not individual clergy. Successful proposals will include a sense of purpose and balance, show evidence that the congregation understands and affirms the value of a renewal program for its leader, and explain the benefit to both the pastor and the congregation.

> National Clergy Renewal Program
> Lilly Endowment Inc.
> P.O. Box 88068
> Indianapolis, IN 46208
> (317) 916-7302
> clergyrenewal@yahoo.com

Video

Oswald, Roy. *Why You Should Give Your Pastor a Sabbatical*. Bethesda, Md.: The Alban Institute, 2001.
A sabbatical offers clergy an opportunity for renewal and lay leaders a time for discovery and growth in their ministry. Roy Oswald makes the compelling argument that a sabbatical is an excellent strategy to help pastors maintain vitality in their work and in communicating the gospel.

A pastoral sabbatical can also be the occasion for lay leaders and members to take a new level of responsibility for pastoral care, congregational oversight, planning and logistics, and other aspects of congregational life traditionally handled by clergy.

Leadership

Books

Callahan, Kennon L. *Effective Church Leadership: Building on the Twelve Keys*. San Francisco: Jossey-Bass, 1990.
   Effective Church Leadership defines and lists the major resources of a missional pastor-leader. The reader will find practical help with the four central tasks of a missional leader: helping people rediscover power in the whole of their lives; helping people become communities of reconciliation; helping people discover meaning in everyday life; and helping people discover how they can make a difference. A plan for pastoral evaluation and an evaluation worksheet are included.

Dawn, Marva J., and Eugene Peterson. *The Unnecessary Pastor: Rediscovering the Call*. Grand Rapids, Mich.: Wm. B. Eerdmans, 1999.
   While the Bible calls pastors to be countercultural servants of Jesus, our culture expects pastors to model goodness, support social stability, and help congregations compete. Marva Dawn and Eugene Peterson remind readers that true Christian leadership must be free of the world's criteria for success. This book will be of particular interest to pastors and lay leaders who feel pulled away from their true call by pressures to fill disparate images of the "ideal" Christian leader.

Hobgood, William Chris. *The Once and Future Pastor: The Changing Role of Religious Leaders*. Bethesda, Md.: The Alban Institute, 1998.
   The emerging church calls for a well-trained pastor, faithful to God's mandate to be a servant leader. Consultant Chris Hobgood describes the characteristics of a church leader. She or he must be spiritually grounded; a trusted and trusting person; hopeful and committed to mission and shared leadership; dedicated to truth-telling; and open to what is happening in the world. This is a helpful, contemporary guide for people selecting and engaged in tomorrow's ministry.

Rice, Howard. *The Pastor as Spiritual Guide*. Nashville: Upper Room Books, 1998.
   As congregations are increasingly compelled to revise their

understandings of pastoral leadership, author Howard Rice believes that "spiritual guidance" is increasingly becoming the pastor's central task. Through spiritual guidance, pastors assist persons who seek meaning in their lives and a vital relationship with God. This study of spiritual guidance as the central authority for ministry and church renewal offers pastors and those who train and support them a way to re-vision the office and the congregation.

Stevens, R. Paul, and Phil Collins. *The Equipping Pastor: A Systems Approach to Congregational Leadership*. Bethesda, Md.: The Alban Institute, 1993. The authors draw on systems theory, covenant relationships, and biblical references to present a convincing model through which clergy can move congregations from focusing on self-preservation to fulfilling their ministry as Christian ambassadors. Shifting the focus from equipping individuals to equipping the whole church, they affirm the importance of interdependence among church members. Although both clergy and laity will benefit from this resource, it is primarily addressed to clergy.

Periodicals

The Clergy Journal. Inver Grove Heights, Minn.: Logos Productions Inc.
The Clergy Journal, targeted to professional clergy, describes itself as a "practical guide to church leadership and personal growth." Published 10 times a year, it features articles that address church administration, ministry issues, personal issues, and preaching and worship resources. The May/June issue is an annual planning issue providing sermons, children's talks, and worship helps for every Sunday of the liturgical church year.

Evaluation

Books

Hudson, Jill M. *Evaluating Ministry: Principles and Processes for Clergy and Congregations*. Bethesda, Md.: The Alban Institute, 1992.
Understanding ministry as mutual and collaborative between congregation and pastorate, Jill Hudson would have any evaluation process apply to both clergy and congregation. For Hudson, evaluation has no connection to problem resolution or conflict management; its purpose centers on growth. The author includes case studies, sample forms and processes,

summaries, and references to denominational guides. She also advocates tailoring one's actual processes to the specific congregation.

Woods, C. Jeff. *User-Friendly Evaluation: Improving the Work of Pastors, Programs, and Laity*. Bethesda, Md.: The Alban Institute, 1995.
User-Friendly Evaluation is perhaps the handiest and most comprehensible survey of evaluation techniques and purposes currently available. For non-professionals approaching the evaluation task, Jeff Woods addresses the questions that are crucial to gathering and using results but that may not have been considered. The book examines the subjects of evaluation programs, lay ministry, and pastoral ministry. Appendices provide three excellent instruments that include guidance on the administration and use of results.

Reports

Clark, Catherine H. *Annual Church Review Procedure: The Church's Ministry and the Minister*. Bethesda, Md.: The Alban Institute, 1986, 2002.
Annual Church Review Procedure provides questionnaire templates that congregations can use to evaluate their ministers, committees, and communities. Most templates include sections for noting accomplishments, rating performance, documenting strengths and weaknesses, and planning and prioritizing future initiatives. Congregations interested in reviewing themselves and their committees, as well as their ministers, will find practical, adaptable tools in this report, available for download from www.alban.org.

Oswald, Roy M. *Getting a Fix on Your Ministry: A Practical Guide to Clergy Performance Appraisal*. Bethesda, Md.: The Alban Institute, 1993, 2002.
Acknowledging the damage that can result from attempts at clergy evaluations, Roy Oswald explains and affirms two evaluation models: a "Ministry Evaluation" model for all church leaders and members; and a "Growth-Oriented Performance Appraisal" model for clergy leaders. Congregations seeking evaluation processes that truly nurture clergy's growth in leadership, lay leaders' growth in effectiveness, and congregations' growth in spiritual maturity will value this special report, available for download from the www.alban.org.

Equipping Lay Ministry

Books

Goetz, David L., editor. *Building Church Leaders: Your Complete Guide to Leadership Training*. Matthews, N.C.: Leadership Journal, 1998.
This looseleaf collection contains reproducible handouts useful for leadership training and discussion on 12 crucial areas of congregational life: assessing church needs; character of a leader; reaching people; church health; spiritual care; handling conflict; recruiting and staffing; finances; motivation leaders; worship; vision; and building a team. Selected by the editors of Leadership Journal, the material comes from leaders such as John Maxwell, Marlene Wilson, Bill Hybels, and others.

Phillips, Roy D. *Letting Go: Transforming Congregations for Ministry*. Bethesda, Md.: The Alban Institute, 1999.
This guide offers a process for moving congregations from a maintenance mindset and likely obsolescence to an attitude of embracing and guiding change. Four major shifts ("letting go") in pastoral and congregational outlook are involved: from membership to ministry; from entitlement to mission; from education to spiritual development; and from toleration to engagement. Questions invite writer-reader interaction, a practical feature for both individuals and groups. Readers of all persuasions will find challenge and encouragement to "let go."

Trumbauer, Jean M. *Created and Called: Discovering Our Gifts for Abundant Living*. Minneapolis: Augsburg Fortress, 1998.
True to its title, *Created and Called* emphasizes that we are co-creators with God in the continuing work of creation and healing, and that each person is gifted and called by the Creator to ministry. Unlike manuals with similar themes, *Created and* Called explains how our gifts are more than our most visible talents and skills. With reflection guides, reflection exercises, samples, and a listing of further resources in each chapter, Jean Trumbauer has provided an excellent resource for gifts identification facilitators to use in small groups, adult education curricula, and leadership programs.

_____. *Sharing the Ministry: A Practical Guide for Transforming Volunteers into Ministers*. Minneapolis: Augsburg Fortress, 1999.
Moving beyond the "fill 'em and forget 'em" volunteer recruitment model, the author presents a new paradigm of volunteer ministry based on the assumptions that each person is uniquely gifted for ministry, that church

ministry is shared, and that staff and lay leaders are to help identify, develop, use, and support the gifts of all members. Trumbauer explains the shared ministry systems model and explores the model's processes. The manual can be used in learning designs for two-session workshops, all-day workshops, or in-service sessions at board, committee, or staff meetings.

Wilson, Marlene. *How to Mobilize Church Volunteers*. Minneapolis: Augsburg, 1983.
Marlene Wilson asserts that church leaders who plan projects and programs should not focus on filling empty volunteer slots; instead, they should identify church members' gifts, leadership styles, and needs. After suggesting guidelines for understanding personality types and improving a church's planning methods and mission goals, she lists exercises for motivating lay members to offer their talents in the church and community. The sample job descriptions, creativity checklist, personal action plan, and evaluation forms provide concrete ways for church members to develop a vibrant model of service.

Change

Books

Bandy, Thomas G. *Moving Off the Map: A Field Guide to Changing the Congregation*. Nashville: Abingdon Press, 1998.
Thomas Bandy argues that only thorough change will save Christian congregations from extinction. This change must be systemic, owned by the congregation, concentrated on the gospel, and anchored in the experience of the congregation with Jesus. The book includes a 280-question Congregational Mission Assessment to help a congregation discern the foundation, function, and form of its life and many practical suggestions for introducing the need for—and effecting—change.

Friedman, Edwin H. *Generation to Generation: Family Process in Church and Synagogue*. New York: Guilford Publications, 1985.
Friedman—for 25 years a congregational rabbi, family therapist, and counselor to clergy of numerous faiths—describes in detail how families in a congregation do and don't work. Throughout, Friedman applies the prism of family systems theory to three "families": the clergy's own family, the congregational family, and families in a congregation. With any family

system, Friedman centers on behavior rather than on labeled individuals, and he demands our attention to process rather than to an "identified problem." This book, packed with theory and example, will repay reading and re-reading over the years.

Markham, Donna J. *Spiritlinking Leadership: Working through Resistance to Organizational Change*. Mahwah, N.J.: Paulist Press, 1999.
Exploring the obstacles that block transformative organizational change, Donna Markham names as "spiritlinking" the courageous leader who finds a way around such obstacles to a future filled with vitality and purpose. With clarity of identity and mission, spiritlinking leaders create synergy, sustain creative conflict, work through grief and resistance, and build collaborative teams in order to move the organization forward to unimagined, creative, new solutions. Questions and practical information at the end of each chapter provide ample material for discussion at retreats, management team meetings, and personal reflection.

Mead, Loren B. *Transforming Congregations for the Future*. Bethesda, Md.: The Alban Institute, 1994.
Showing that mainline denominations have lost members and money during the past three decades, Loren Mead asks that we dedicate ourselves not merely to increased numbers, but to congregational transformation. A transformed congregation nurtures and strengthens its members' discipleship through building community, proclaiming God's Word, teaching sacred stories, and discovering and developing gifts of service. Offering both inspiration and a realistic appraisal of the roadblocks to transformation, this book will challenge congregational and judicatory leaders to re-envision themselves and their tasks.

Rendle, Gilbert R. *Leading Change in the Congregation: Spiritual and Organizational Tools for Leaders*. Bethesda, Md.: The Alban Institute, 1998.
This practical guide is for congregational leaders trying to be faithful in a turbulent and unpredictable environment. It combines theory, research, and the author's experience to provide leaders and others with practical diagnostic models and tools for leading change in a spiritual way. The case studies, analyses, worksheets, and games included in this book will help congregations and their leaders undertand the varied reactions that change can elicit.

Senge, Peter M., Art Kleiner, Charlotte Roberts, Richard Ross, George Roth, and Bryan Smith. *The Dance of Change: The Challenges to Sustaining Momentum in Learning Organizations*. New York: Doubleday, 1999.

Peter Senge and others apply systems theory to the leadership task of starting and sustaining productive, developmental life in organizations. The reader can divide the book into three parts: (1) the overarching theory, and most essential definitions, in the first two chapters; (2) the "big picture" overview at the end; (3) the rest of the book, which elaborates the limiting processes that shape profound change. With its useful attention to behaviors and attitudes that constrain and derail the development of an institution and its members, this book is bedrock material for leaders in any field.

Conflict

Books

Halstead, Kenneth A. *From Stuck to Unstuck: Overcoming Congregational Impasse*. Bethesda, Md.: The Alban Institute, 1998.
   Drawing on his experience as a pastor and counselor, Kenneth Halstead suggests that systems theory concepts and brief therapy interventions may help to resolve congregational impasses. He envisions a new leadership paradigm of creative cooperation, mutual empowerment, and trustful caring to replace the old model of competition for control and caretaking. Pastors, denominational leaders, conflict management professionals, and church leaders can benefit from Halstead's suggestions for churches to move forward in ministry.

Hobgood, William C. *Welcoming Resistance*. Bethesda, Md.: The Alban Institute, 2001.
   Exploring the types, bases, and processes of change, Welcoming Resistance encourages readers to understand resistance in a congregation's mission-focused work. William Hobgood describes kinds of resistance, the interests undergirding resistance, and the levels of leadership initiative that call forth corresponding levels of resistance. After presenting eight condensed case studies, the book concludes with a definition of the "initiative/resistance" cycle and some "rules" for managing congregational initiatives and resistance.

Leas, Speed B. *Discover Your Conflict Management* Style. Bethesda, Md.: The Alban Institute, 1997.
   Speed Leas, an Alban Institute senior consultant and well-known expert on congregational conflict, developed the 45-question self-administered

"conflict inventory" included in this book to help people learn about their styles of managing conflict—before they become involved in a conflict situation. He describes the styles—persuading, compelling, avoiding/accommodating, collaborating, negotiating, and supporting— and discusses the pros and cons of each. The goal of the book is to give people better access to the vocabulary of conflict and insight into how they behave when conflicts arise.

Lott, David B., ed. *Conflict Management in Congregations*. Bethesda, Md.: The Alban Institute, 2001.
This compilation volume, comprised of 20 classic essays, harvests the collected wisdom of a dozen key thinkers on conflict management issues. Divided into three sections on the dynamics of conflict, conflict management techniques, and dealing with conflict in specific contexts, the book serves as a basic primer on the topic. Featuring a new introduction by Speed B. Leas on how thinking about conflict managment has changed, additional authors include David Augsburger, Alice Mann, George Parsons, Gil Rendle, and Caroline Westerhoff.

Rendle, Gilbert R. *Behavioral Covenants in Congregations: A Handbook for Honoring Differences*. Bethesda, Md.: The Alban Institute, 1999.
Behavioral Covenants in Congregations offers congregations an approach to managing their differences with maturity and respect. Challenging congregations to practice those behaviors that reflect the standards of their faith, Gil Rendle offers the behavioral covenant as a useful approach to answering a key question: "How will we behave when we don't understand each other and when we don't agree?" The book provides modules for developing behavioral covenants in leadership retreats, committee meetings, and leadership team meetings, as well as examples of various covenants.

Stone, Douglas, Bruce Patton, and Sheila Heen. *Difficult Conversations: How to Discuss What Matters Most*. New York: Penguin Books, 1999.
Difficult Conversations offers an approach to those often conflict-ridden conversations we find most painful and tend to avoid. The book suggests ways to prepare for a difficult conversation, determine one's purposes, start such a conversation, explore each person's stories and viewpoints, and begin the problem-solving process. Concluding with a "difficult conversations checklist" and organizational bibliography, *Difficult Conversations* is a must-read for leaders who seek to move congregational conflicts from a "blame game" to an opportunity for mutual understanding.

Welcome to the work of Alban Institute...
the leading publisher and congregational
resource organization for clergy and laity today.

Your purchase of this book means you have an interest in the kinds of information, research, consulting, networking opportunities and educational seminars that Alban Institute produces and provides. We are a non-denominational, non-profit 25-year-old membership organization dedicated to providing practical and useful support to religious congregations and those who participate in and lead them.

Alban is acknowledged as a pioneer in learning and teaching on *Conflict Management *Faith and Money *Congregational Growth and Change *Leadership Development *Mission and Planning *Clergy Recruitment and Training *Clergy Support, Self-Care and Transition *Spirituality and Faith Development *Congregational Security.

Our membership is comprised of over 8,000 clergy, lay leaders, congregations and institutions who benefit from:

❖ 15% discount on hundreds of Alban books
❖ $50 per-course tuition discount on education seminars
❖ Subscription to *Congregations*, the Alban journal (a $30 value)
❖ Access to Alban research and (soon) the "Members-Only" archival section of our web site www.alban.org

For more information on Alban membership or to be added to our catalog mailing list, call 1-800-486-1318, ext.243 or return this form.

Name and Title: _____

Congregation/Organization: _____

Address: _____

City: _____ Tel.: _____

State: _____ Zip: _____ Email: _____

BKIN

The Alban Institute
Attn: Membership Dept.
7315 Wisconsin Avenue
Suite 1250 West
Bethesda, MD 20814-3211

This book is made possible in part by the fees the Alban Institute charges for our products and services. The cost to produce our products and services is greater than the prices we ask. Therefore, we depend on the generous support of foundations, individual, congregational, and institutional members of the Institute, and friends like you, which enables us to continue to develop and make available our resources at less than their full cost.

We invite you to add your support to that of this generous group of friends who believe that the vitality of our religious communities and congregations is of the utmost importance.

To learn more about the Alban Institute and to contribute to our efforts, please visit us online: www.alban.org.

THE
ALBAN
INSTITUTE